AGILITY TRAINING

AGILITY TRAINING

The Fun Sport for All Dogs

Jane Simmons-Moake

HOWELL
BOOK HOUSE

MACMILLAN • USA

Macmillan General Reference
A Simon & Schuster Macmillan Company
1633 Broadway
New York, NY 10019-6785

Agility Dog[SM], Advanced Agility Dog[SM], Master Agility Dog[SM] and Grand Prix of Dog Agility[SM] are the exclusive service marks of the United States Dog Agility Association, Inc.

Library of Congress Cataloging-in-Publication Data
Simmons-Moake, Jane.
    Agility training: the fun sport for all dogs / Jane Simmons-Moake.
      p.   cm.
    ISBN 0-87605-402-5
    1. Dogs—Agility trials.   2. Dogs—Training.   I. Title.
    SF425.4.S56   1992
    636.7'088—dc20   91-22676
                                                            CIP

20   19   18   17   16   15   14   13

Printed in the United States of America

To Pandora, my first Agility dog, whose enthusiasm for the sport sparked my passion for Agility. And to all the dogs at FlashPaws, whose accomplishments and wagging tails are a continuing inspiration.

Contents

Acknowledgments

I COULD NOT have written this book without the generous help of many others, to whom I am sincerely grateful:

- My good friend Cindy Lottinville —thank you for your valuable review comments and for helping to implement the methods in this book.

- My friends Lisa Layton, John Lottinville and Liby Messler, who provided invaluable insight and perspective.

- Special thanks to Liby for her *superb* work on many of the illustrations that appear thoughout the book.

- Our students at *FlashPaws*, from whom I learn something new every day.

- My faithful companions Pandy, Tracy and Spirit, who kept my feet warm while I labored at the computer.

- My husband, Gordon, cofounder of *FlashPaws* and codeveloper of many of the methods described within these pages, as well as the writer of the Obstacle Construction Appendix. No one could ask for a better husband, friend or training partner!

Jane Simmons-Moake.

Photo: Robert Hebert

About the Author

JANE SIMMONS-MOAKE became involved in Agility in 1986, soon after the sport was introduced to this country. After years of training in competitive Obedience and earning numerous Obedience titles, she and her husband Gordon decided that their dogs deserved to participate in the more "fun" outlets of dog training: Flyball, Scent Hurdles and Agility. Agility became their special area of interest as they discovered how much fun it could be for both the dog and the handler.

To share their knowledge and enthusiasm for the sport, they founded the *FlashPaws* Agility Training Center, which has since helped hundreds of dogs and handlers discover the excitement of Agility training and is the training ground for many top Agility competitors in the nation.

One of the country's foremost Agility trainers and competitors, Ms. Simmons-Moake has owned and trained the number one Agility Golden Retriever in the United States—U-CDX Rimrac's Opalescence, UD, FDCh, AD. "Pandy" also finished among the top ten in all-breed competition at the USDAA National Finals in 1990.

Jane and Gordon Simmons-Moake were two of the country's first licensed Agility judges. As respected "old-timers" in this relatively young sport, they are often called upon for training and obstacle construction advice by new Agility groups throughout the country.

Ms. Simmons-Moake holds an M.S. and an Ed.S. in Instructional Technology and is a training consultant and instructional author. Mr. Simmons-Moake holds a Ph.D. in Nuclear Physics and conducts research for the oil and gas industries.

Preface

THIS BOOK is intended for anyone interested in Agility, whether that interest is purely casual and recreational, moderately competitive or highly competitive. The chapters and methods that will be most meaningful to you depend upon your Agility goals.

The training methods in this book can best be described as "a practical approach." My approach is practical because it can be used by average people with busy lives. Within these chapters, you'll find practical techniques for handlers with limited training time, as well as more training-intensive techniques for those who are striving for a competitive edge.

Having taught hundreds of participants in our Agility classes, it became overwhelmingly apparent that people are drawn to Agility first and foremost as a way to have fun with their dogs. I learned quickly that not everyone has the desire or the determination to train hard to win. However, it's also true that many people who start out with humble aspirations and a half-hearted commitment get a taste of success and are inspired to heighten their goals for achievement.

Whatever your goals, the key element is *fun* for you and your four-legged partner. Keep this in mind and you'll always have a winning team.

AGILITY TRAINING

Agility is simply the most fun and exciting activity you can share with your dog!
Photo: Gene Abrahamson

1

About Agility—
What It Is, Who Does It
and Why

SIMPLY PUT, Agility is the most fun you can share with your dog! In its recreational form, Agility is like a visit to a doggy amusement park, providing an outlet for excess energy and a fun way to spend some free time with your canine companion. In its competitive form, Agility is the up-and-coming dog sport in which dogs traverse a maze of obstacles and compete for speed and accuracy. Racing against the clock, dogs jump through tires, zip through tunnels, scale a 6-foot-tall A-frame, traverse a narrow "dog walk," negotiate a see-saw, zig-zag through closely spaced, upright poles and soar over a variety of challenging hurdles—all at great speed.

Agility as a spectator sport began in Great Britain in 1978 with a small-scale demonstration at Crufts, considered by many to be the most prestigious dog show in the world. The show committee wanted an entertaining diversion to fill the spare time between the Obedience championships and the Group judging held in the main arena, so John Varley and Peter Meanwell conceived the notion of dog Agility—a challenging obstacle course with many elements borrowed from equestrian events. The demonstration had overwhelming spectator appeal, largely because of the fast pace, the challenging and visually spectacular obstacles and the contagious enthusiasm displayed by the dogs. Within a year and a half, the Kennel Club gave Agility its blessing, adopted a set of regulations and began offering Agility as a regular competitive event.

Today, Agility enjoys enormous popularity in Britain, with well-attended competitions every weekend during the show season. The larger events draw thousands of competitors and attract huge, appreciative audiences—many competitions are even televised! This enthusiasm for Agility has spread to virtually all of Europe, as well as Australia and New Zealand, thus making Agility a truly international dog sport.

The United States caught this wind of excitement in the early 1980s. In 1986, Kenneth Tatsch founded the United States Dog Agility Association (USDAA), dedicated to preserving international standards in anticipation of worldwide competitive events. The USDAA patterns its rules and obstacles after British Agility to provide the same spectator appeal and enthusiasm enjoyed overseas.

In 1990, the USDAA began awarding Agility titles—certifications of accomplishment at different levels that award you the privilege of adding letters after your dog's name (similar to college degrees). The first level of achievement is Agility Dog^{SM} (AD), followed by Advanced Agility Dog^{SM} (AAD) and Master Agility Dog^{SM} (MAD). *All dogs, including mixed breeds, are eligible to earn titles.*

Since 1986, participation in the sport has grown tremendously, partly because of this new opportunity to earn titles. Another large factor has been increased public exposure as more and more Agility events have become a highly visible part of some of the nation's largest dog shows and equestrian events.

Another form of Agility was created in 1987 by Charles "Bud" Kramer, founder of the National Club (formerly Committee) for Dog Agility (NCDA). This version of Agility was designed to be easily portable and to be set up in small locations with limited ring space. These obstacles are constructed primarily of plastic (with some steel reinforcement), the planks are wider and the hurdles, dog walk and A-frame are lower. The required speed is slower, and events are relatively noncompetitive. Because of the ease of mastery and small space requirements, NCDA Agility has been adopted in some areas of the country. You may find this style of Agility meets your goals if you desire a low-key approach.

If you train using the British-style equipment, you can also participate in NCDA Agility (and do quite well!) should the opportunity present itself. Because of speed requirements and equipment size, those who train only using the NCDA equipment usually are not able to participate in British-style Agility, which is currently more widespread. For these reasons, this book focuses on training using British-style obstacles and rules like those used by the USDAA.

WHY DO AGILITY?

People are attracted to Agility for a wide variety of reasons. Some simply want to spend some "quality time" with their dogs doing something that's fun

Two styles of Agility obstacles: NCDA (*above*) and USDAA (*below*).

3

Why Agility? Because it's just plain fun!

together. The only thing that is more fun than watching dogs do Agility is doing it with your own dog.

Agility is great for dogs that have become bored with other forms of dog training, such as competitive obedience. Some worry that their dogs will love Agility training so much that their attitudes will worsen toward Obedience training. What usually happens, however, is that the dogs' attitudes toward obedience work actually improve as a result of the positive working relationship created through Agility training.

Owners of breeds not typically found in the Obedience ring are drawn to Agility as a way to have fun while displaying the capabilities and versatility of their breeds. This highly visible spectator sport is a fine showcase to display spark, intelligence and an attitude of teamwork.

Some dog owners who begin Agility work have no intention of competing in Agility trials—they see Agility as a means of instilling confidence in their dogs, to enhance their performance in breed or obedience competition or to make their dogs more confident pets.

"Mookie," a Belgian Sheepdog, had been afraid to climb stairs all his life. After several weeks of Agility obstacle training, Mookie shocked and delighted his owner by voluntarily climbing the stairs by himself. "Annie," a sweet but somewhat insecure Doberman Pinscher, impressed her friends at the yacht club when her Agility training gave her the confidence to jump from the dock to the deck of the boat and even to walk along the boat's narrow ledges and ramps.

Some dog owners enroll in Agility as a way to help their active canines "blow off steam" in a constructive and pleasurable manner. "Morgan," a lovable but rambunctious mixed breed, was a destructive chewer. An only dog with an owner who worked during the day, Morgan couldn't help using some of his excess energy to nibble away on the carpet in the room in which he was confined. When his "mom" returned from work to discover his handiwork, she did not feel much like throwing the ball or taking the lad for a run in the park. As a result, both Morgan and mom grew more frustrated and their relationship (and home furnishings) suffered. Then they discovered Agility—a mother approved outlet for venting canine energy. Morgan took to Agility immediately, as if it were something he was "meant to do." Morgan's owner surprised herself by how much she enjoyed the training sessions—for the first time seeing her unruly friend turn into a willing and appreciative teammate. The destructive chewing stopped, and a stronger relationship was born.

WHAT DOGS CAN DO AGILITY?

Almost any physically and mentally sound dog can enjoy Agility. In fact, we've seen many "unlikely" breeds happily making tracks around the Agility course—including Basset Hounds, Pugs and Corgis.

Shasta, a Great Pyrenees, clears
the spread-bar jump at full height.

A few giant breeds such as Great Danes, Mastiffs and Newfoundlands may find the openings in the tire and tunnels too small to fit through, which may prevent them from competing on standard equipment. This doesn't mean, however, that these breeds can't participate for fun on larger equipment. On the other hand, we have had breeds such as Borzois, Great Pyrenees and Irish Wolfhounds in our classes that did learn to do all the Standard competition obstacles. In many of these cases the dogs appeared reluctant at first, but after overcoming the initial concern, performed reliably and seemed proud of their accomplishments. So did their owners!

One of the most heartwarming experiences in Agility that I can recall involved a one-hundred-pound Great Pyrenees named Shasta. Shasta, despite his tremendous size, always performed the tunnels and contact obstacles with style and enthusiasm. Hurdles, on the other hand, were a problem. Even at a low height it always seemed a struggle for Shasta to send his massive body over the hurdles. As a result, Shasta's handler assumed he would never be able to physically clear a 30-inch spread-bar jump. One day after class, since we had all worked together for some time, we let the dogs run around and chase each other to blow off steam. It was a cold day and Shasta was moving faster than I'd ever seen him move. Imagine our shock and delight when in the course of playing with his friends, Shasta cleanly and confidently cleared a 30-inch spread-bar jump that happened to be in his path!

Purely by accident we learned that Shasta was physically capable of per-

Watson, an OTCH Bichon Frise, clears the spread-bar jump with ease.

forming the jump with ease and that jumping wasn't something he disliked. We also learned to never underestimate the capabilities of our dogs—they have a way of living up to our expectations!

Although owners of some giant breeds have valid concerns, no dog is too small to enjoy and excel in Agility. We have yet to encounter a small dog that couldn't negotiate all the obstacles successfully. In fact, in our beginner classes, most Toy breeds can reliably jump their full height on the first night of class! This is never the case for large dogs unless they have had previous training in jumping.

Unsuitable for Agility are extremely overweight dogs, dogs with physical disabilities such as poor vision or lameness, or dogs with mental handicaps such as extreme spookiness or tactile sensitivity.

Young puppies think planks are great fun.

2

Getting Started

So, YOU THINK THAT Agility might be fun and you'd like to give it a try. How do you get started? The easiest way is to enroll in classes at an Agility training center or join a local Agility training club. To find a group in your area, call around to several schools that teach Obedience classes. They will usually know who is training Agility. If your search comes up negative, this presents you with a unique opportunity—to be the first in your area to start training Agility!

AGE

You'll hear many different philosophies about the proper age to start training a dog for Agility, and the best answer is "at whatever age you feel most comfortable." Those who prefer to wait until the dog is full grown are most likely concerned that the dog will sustain an injury from a fall while the bones and joints are not fully mature. However, you can avoid such accidents with proper training techniques—puppies should simply *never* fall off equipment!

We've found that the earlier you introduce puppies to the obstacles, the better their attitude and aptitude will be when they're grown. Seven-week-old puppies can learn to love racing through tunnels and can learn the dog walk, see-saw and a flattened A-frame. The dog gains confidence while having fun in constructive play. Because puppies are often fearless and may try to run too fast over the dog walk, cross-over and see-saw, make sure the puppy *never* falls. You can ensure safety while your puppy traverses the obstacle by placing your hands on either side of the pup or by having a reliable spotter on each side.

During the first year of life, a puppy's bones and joints are developing, so jumping should be restricted to elbow height or lower. You should also refrain from intensive drilling. You need not be in a hurry since dogs are not permitted to compete in Agility trials until they are twelve months old. Even with very limited practice in jumping, a puppy can learn to respond to the jump command and can learn control and sequencing, all at a very low, safe height. Full-height jumping can begin when the dog is twelve to fifteen months old, depending on the breed.

Whether you want a future Agility champion or a well-mannered household pet, your puppy can benefit from motivational obedience training upon becoming part of your household. Using food or toys and a generous amount of praise, you can teach your puppy to respond enthusiastically to your first commands to sit, stay, down and the all-important come—commands that your puppy will need for advanced Agility training.

CHOOSING A FUTURE AGILITY CHAMPION

For most people, choosing a dog for Agility is not an issue. You already have a dog and want to engage in a fun and exciting activity. This is exactly as it should be. Agility can be addicting, however, and if you're bitten by the "bug" and have decided to acquire a dog for the purpose of doing Agility, choose a dog with mental and physical "Agility potential" in mind.

Temperament

Agility has been known to improve some dogs' temperaments. A shy, timid or spooky dog can sometimes become more outgoing with a newfound confidence after learning to negotiate the obstacles. However, if you're looking for a future Agility star in a puppy, don't gamble on one that is spooky or timid—choose one with an optimum temperament to begin with. That is, choose a confident, outgoing, energetic, curious puppy that doesn't have noise or tactile sensitivities.

Choose an outgoing puppy—one that happily approaches strangers and follows them as they walk away. Avoid puppies that seem overly fearful or indifferent. The pup should be curious about its surroundings and should readily approach unfamiliar objects. Avoid puppies that are overly noise-sensitive. To test noise sensitivity and curiosity, place some metal objects such as coins or hardware in an empty coffee can. Shake it hard, then roll it on the floor. Look for a puppy that does not appear fearful and confidently approaches the can to investigate the sound.

Look for a puppy that readily walks on its own on strange surfaces. Place unusual textures on the ground such as plastic sheeting, metal grating, boards and poles. A dog that refuses to walk on strange surfaces after gentle encour-

In your search for a future Agility champion, choose an outgoing, curious and confident puppy.

agement may be tactile-sensitive and may be resistant to walking through tunnels or over the contact obstacles.

If you ask ten different trainers you'll most likely get ten different opinions about what special qualities to look for beyond the basic characteristics of sound temperament. Personally, I place a great deal of emphasis on a dog's natural ability to "focus"—both on me and on the task at hand. A hyper, bouncing-off-the-wall puppy may be able to perform all day, but may also take the patience of a saint and loads of extra work to get focused on the tasks of my choosing. One way I test focus is to do a simple retrieve test. In a room with the door closed and free from distractions, get the puppy's attention with a wad of crumpled paper and throw it a short distance. A dog that ignores the toss, even after several tries at several different sessions when *you are sure* the pup has seen the paper, has less than ideal focus. Some of these dogs have a "fawning" personality and will lick and jump on you rather than go after the paper. Some will ignore your retrieve object and go off exploring on their own. A dog with good innate focus will repeatedly go after the tossed object. If the dog picks it up—even better. If the pup brings it back—better yet!

Physical Characteristics

Agility is a strenuous activity for dogs—and physical soundness is essential if your dog is to hold up to the running, jumping and climbing required by the

Agility is a strenuous activity for dogs; therefore, physical soundness is essential.

sport. Among the most important physical characteristics your dog needs are sound hips, good eyesight and a strong, healthy heart. Unfortunately, some breeds experience high incidences of hip dysplasia (a crippling malformation of the hip joint), eye diseases and heart problems. Many of these defects are genetic, passed on from parents to offspring, usually as a result of indiscriminate breeding practices.

It seems the more popularity a breed enjoys, the more often unscrupulous or ignorant breeders produce puppies with no thought given to perpetuating genetic defects. Since these defects are often undetectable in puppies, there is no way of knowing if the dog will experience problems when older and already a cherished member of your family. The best you can do is to acquire your puppy from a litter in which both parents have been screened for any genetic defects present in your breed. Although screening doesn't guarantee your puppy will be sound, it increases your chances significantly. If you are looking for a member of a popular breed and want to know what genetic defects are present and screened for, contact a national or local breed club. They can usually provide you with the literature or information you need.

When choosing between different puppies of a single breed, you must always keep your priorities in mind. Although the heavier-boned, stockier puppy may be more physically attractive and may fare better in conformation competition, a lighter-boned, leggier littermate will probably be quicker, more agile and a better jumper, and have more stamina (if all other physical and mental factors are equal). Other physical characteristics to consider include balanced structure (with well-matched front and rear angulation) and overall coordination.

Dog Size and Shape: Advantages and Disadvantages

As we have said, all dogs can enjoy Agility, so it makes the most sense to choose a breed or mix that fits your preferences and life-style, rather than one that was "born to do Agility." A good trainer can get results with any mentally and physically sound dog, and for most people it is enough to set their goals at excelling among others who train their same breed.

It makes sense, however, that some breeds have characteristics that make them more naturally suited to Agility than others. The greatest competitive potential comes from breeds that are quick, agile, intelligent, tireless jumpers and willing workers. Because of their light weight, relatively long legs, intelligence and obsession for work, Border Collies are the outstanding breed for Agility, as many enthusiasts have discovered.

Dogs of all sizes can be competitive in Agility, so it makes sense to choose a size of dog that suits your life-style. However, it helps to be aware of the different challenges facing trainers of different sized dogs.

Small dogs have distinct advantages in some areas and distinct disadvantages in others. Rarely do small dogs miss contact zones (obstacle areas that dogs must touch) since the contact zones are several times longer than the dog. This frees their handlers from concentrating on controlling contact zones either in training or while running a course. They can also take a more cavalier approach to controlling their dogs between obstacles—the timing of commands is not as critical since a small dog takes several strides between obstacles and does not require a long, head-on approach. For this reason small dogs can take a shorter path around the course than large dogs, effectively shortening the number of yards they are required to run. Small dogs do, however, have more difficulty negotiating the A-frame and cannot cover the ground as quickly as some of the larger breeds. Speed only becomes a limiting factor, though, at higher levels of competition where the Standard Course Times are fast. Still, a fast small dog can be very competitive.

Good news for small-dog owners, the double-bar jump requirements have been recently lowered for dogs in the 12-inch and 18-inch height categories. Instead of both bars of the double-bar jump being placed at the maximum height, one bar has been lowered to a height of 6 inches to make it easy for even the smallest of dogs.

Large dogs have an advantage in that they can cover ground quickly, but that is where the advantages end—in fact, a large, fast dog is more likely to

Dogs of all sizes love
Agility.

14

miss obstacle contact zones than a slower, more deliberate dog. Handlers of large dogs must resign themselves to dealing with contact zones problems both in training and during competition. Large-dog handlers must also be more accurate in the timing of commands since there are often only one or two strides between obstacles. A late command can give your dog insufficient preparation to approach the next obstacle, or insufficient warning to call it off an incorrect obstacle in its path. Because of their size, large dogs must work harder to bend their bodies through the weave poles, must be more accurate to fit inside the pause box without hanging out of it, and are more often subject to penalties for overshooting the pause table.

Medium-sized dogs are usually the most competitive—they have less of a problem with safety zones than do large dogs and have fewer problems reaching competitive speeds than do most small dogs. In fact, many medium-sized dogs cover ground much more quickly than larger dogs.

Socialization

After you select your puppy, go to as many indoor and outdoor places as possible for exposure to a multitude of sights and sounds while the pup is young. Carry food treats in your pocket and ask strangers to pet and feed your puppy, making sure all new experiences are pleasant.

Nothing is more frustrating than having a dog that is trained to perfection on your own training ground but can't perform in public because of a dislike or fear of dog shows. Dog shows can be crowded and noisy with barking dogs, cheering crowds, and loud PA systems. To help ensure that your pup learns to love going to shows, it's best to expose your puppy to them while young. Unfortunately, many shows prohibit puppies under the age of six months on show grounds.

To get around this problem, you can bring the dog show to your home! Take a tape recorder with you to the next few local dog shows and stash it in the noisiest place you can find; then go enjoy the show. When you've collected a good assortment of sounds, play the tape during your puppy's meal time—quietly at first, then with gradually increasing volume over a period of days. When your puppy is old enough to attend the first show, the sounds will be familiar and even pleasurable.

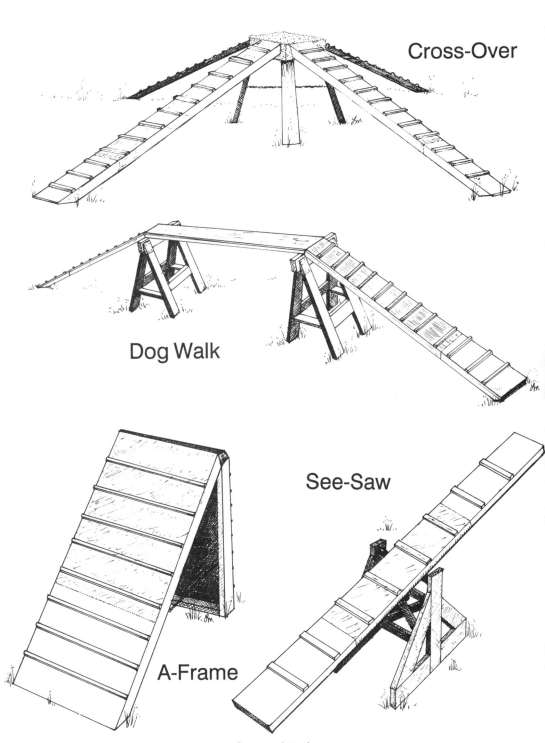

Cross-Over

Dog Walk

See-Saw

A-Frame

Contact obstacles.

16

3

Obstacle Training

OBSTACLE TRAINING is the first—and, believe it or not, the simplest—part of Agility training. If your goal is recreation rather than competition, you need go no further in your training than teaching the individual obstacles. You'll enjoy the rewarding experience of helping your dog succeed and gain newfound confidence—some dogs become especially proud of themselves! For those who continue their training, this is just the first of many bigger rewards. You'll experience the thrill of finely tuned teamwork as you direct your dog to traverse a complicated maze of obstacles with enthusiasm and accuracy —when your dog isn't even wearing a collar!

Whether training for competition, confidence building or companionship, both you and your dog should look forward to your Agility training sessions. Our students tell us their dogs know when it's "Agility night"—the dogs become restless, eagerly hop in the car and get more and more excited as they get closer to the training center. To elicit this type of excitement and energy from your dog, it's important that your attitude be positive and enthusiastic from the start. This means leaving the day's frustrations behind the moment you pick up the lead, resolving yourself to be fair and patient and being prepared to make a fool out of yourself by abundantly praising whenever your dog does something particularly wonderful.

OBSTACLES—A DEFINITION

The Agility obstacles are divided into several categories: contact obstacles, tunnels, hurdles, weave poles, pause obstacles and the tire jump.

17

Contact Obstacles

The contact obstacles consist of the *see-saw, A-frame, dog walk* and *cross-over*. All are similar in that the dog must climb and descend inclined planks. Contact obstacles have yellow painted ends, which are "safety zones" or "contact zones," intended to prevent dogs from jumping off an obstacle too early and possibly sustaining an injury. When traversing a contact obstacle, the dog must touch each of the yellow contact zones with at least one foot to avoid penalties or "faults." Faults are accumulated during your dog's entire course "run" and work against the final score.

The cross-over, an **X**-shaped obstacle with four 12-foot planks converging on an elevated platform, provides an added challenge. The dog must ascend and descend the planks indicated by the judge's course design, either making a left turn, making a right turn or continuing straight across. Dogs are penalized for taking an incorrect plank.

Tunnels

There are two types of tunnels on the Agility course. The *pipe tunnel* is an open tube that is bendable into a variety of shapes and configurations, whereas

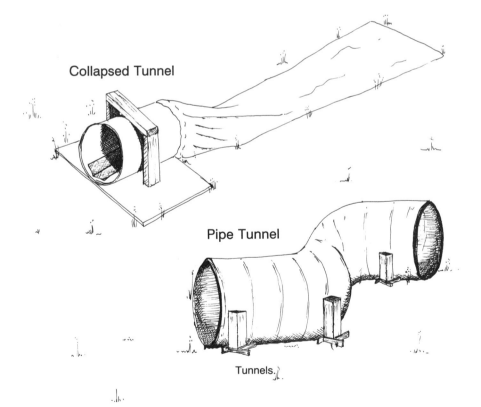

Collapsed Tunnel

Pipe Tunnel

Tunnels.

18

the *collapsed tunnel* consists of a rigid opening followed by a 12-foot fabric chute through which the dog must burrow. The tunnels are among the easiest obstacles to train and tend to be naturally fun for den animals such as dogs— so much fun that it can be a challenge to keep them out of the tunnels when you want them to go elsewhere!

Hurdles

Hurdles are obstacles that test your dog's ability to jump. Some hurdles require the dog to jump high, some to jump wide and some require a jump both high and wide. The height and width of the hurdles varies with the height of the dog.

The hurdles comprise a large percentage of the obstacles on the course and assume a wide variety of forms. Commonly used hurdles are:

- single-bar jump
- double-bar jump
- spread-bar jump (sometimes called the triple-bar jump)
- long jump
- barrel jump
- bone jump

Some groups have added fan jumps, lattice jumps, wall jumps and water jumps for variety.

Almost any type of hurdle is acceptable as long as it meets prescribed size requirements and has a displaceable top bar or board. This way, if the dog hits the top of the hurdle while jumping, the bar or board will fall away, helping to prevent injuries. In competition whenever the dog knocks down a bar or board, faults are incurred.

The height a dog will be required to jump in competition is based on the dog's height at the shoulder. As of this writing there are four jump-height categories. 12 inches, 18 inches, 24 inches and 30 inches. Dogs 12 inches and under jump 12 inches, dogs over 12 inches through 16 inches jump 18 inches, dogs over 16 inches through 21 inches jump 24 inches and dogs over 21 inches jump 30 inches high.

The ''long jump'' (sometimes called a broad jump) requires the dog to jump wide rather than high. Dogs in the 12-inch height category jump a long jump width of 20 inches. For the other height categories, the width of the spread is twice the dog's jump height; therefore, the spread widths for the 18-inch, 24-inch and 30-inch height categories are 36 inches, 48 inches and 60 inches respectively. To receive credit for performing the long jump properly, the dog must enter and exit between both sets of corner poles.

Like other aspects of our rapidly growing and evolving sport, jump heights and widths are always subject to change. To illustrate, at one time there were four jump heights. This rapidly changed to three. Then, in 1991, four jump

Hurdles.

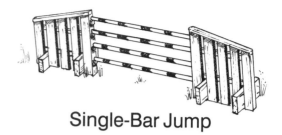

Single-Bar Jump

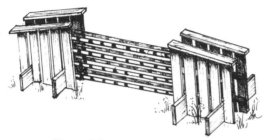

Double-Bar Jump

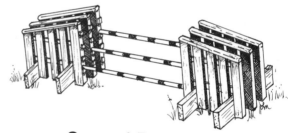

Spread-Bar Jump

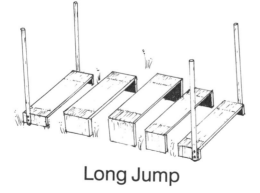

Long Jump

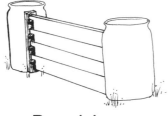

Barrel Jump

Bone Jump

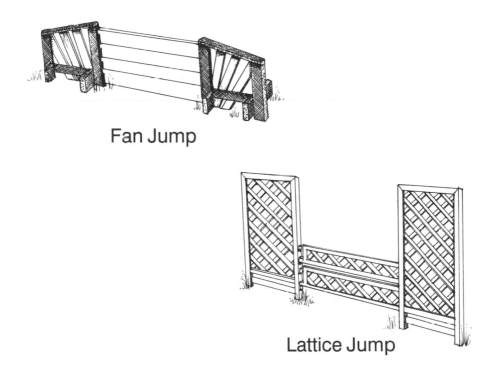

Fan Jump

Lattice Jump

heights were reinstated. (This explains why some of the photographs in this book show dogs performing hurdles that are adjustable to only three different jump heights.)

Weave Poles

The weave poles are two sets of upright poles through which the dog must serpentine quickly and accurately. Although the weave pole construction specifications can vary within published guidelines, most Agility-training groups have standardized on two sets of five poles spaced 20 inches apart. The two sets may be used separately or together to form one set of poles. To perform the poles properly, the dog must enter to the right of the first pole and continue weaving in and out without skipping a pole. Improper entry and skipped poles may be faulted in competition. Weave poles require a good deal of practice to learn but, once mastered, are a thrill for the dog as well as the spectator.

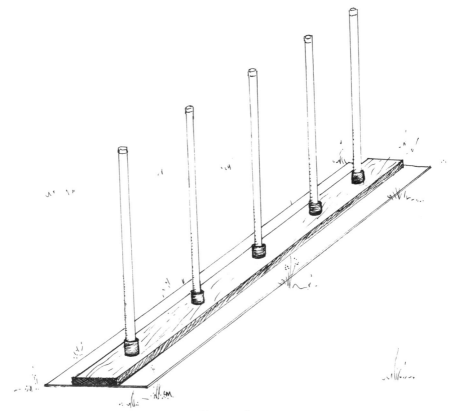

Weave poles.

Pause Obstacles

The pause obstacles include the *pause table* and the *pause box*, the latter being used relatively infrequently. The dog must jump on the pause table or stop inside the pause box and assume the down position for a period of five seconds. All dogs use the same pause box regardless of the size of the dog. The height of the pause table varies, however, based on the jump height of the dog. A dog is never required to perform a pause table that is higher than its jump height.

In competition, faults are assessed if a dog slides or jumps off the pause table (or runs out of the pause box) or if the dog anticipates the release before the five seconds have elapsed.

Tire Jump

The tire jump consists of a tire suspended from a frame at a height that corresponds with the dog's established jump height. This obstacle is not considered just another type of hurdle since the dog must jump through a narrow circular opening suspended in midair. For larger dogs especially, negotiating the tire jump demands precision, timing and confidence.

USING REWARDS

Many dogs find Agility so exciting they need only your praise and approval to keep them motivated to try the new things presented in training. For others, food or toys can help attract and hold interest, and can help dogs overcome any

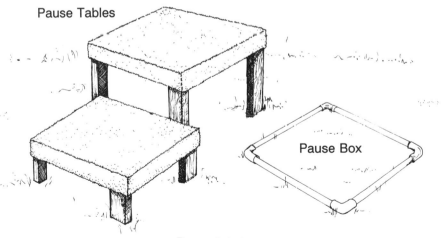

Pause Tables

Pause Box

Pause obstacles.

A reward is anything your dog really enjoys. This dog works for pine cones.

hesitation or fear associated with learning something new. As the dog gains confidence, you will need to rely less on food and toys, using them only intermittently for reinforcement.

When introducing a new obstacle to a dog that is reluctant to try it, or is unsure of what you want, you can show a treat or a toy as an incentive (or bribe). Once the dog is familiar with the obstacle, discontinue the bribe and use the treat or toy as a reward that you magically pull out of your pocket after each successful performance. Couple the reward with a sincerely delivered "praise phrase" such as "Good dog!" After your dog has mastered the obstacle, reward your dog only randomly. Doing so will encourage motivation since the dog never knows when a reward will be given.

When using praise and tangible rewards to reinforce desired behavior while teaching a new exercise, it's important that you time your praise and give the reward *immediately following* the correct behavior. Praise should be given within a fraction of a second, and the reward should follow as soon as possible. A bait pouch or tennis ball clip can be hung on your belt to keep your rewards handy, while freeing your hands for signals and congratulatory hugs.

WRONG IS ALL RIGHT

Every dog makes honest mistakes when learning something new—it is actually a necessary part of learning. When these mistakes occur, do your best to maintain a positive attitude. Repeat the exercise, making sure you do not allow the dog to make the same mistake twice. This may mean putting the dog back on-lead (if now off-lead) or putting up physical barriers to prevent your dog from repeating the incorrect behavior. If you allow the dog to make the same mistake repeatedly, you pattern the wrong behavior—in essence, you teach the dog to perform incorrectly. When this happens, you must then reteach the behavior, which is much more difficult than teaching it correctly in the first place. Couple a successful performance with immediate, effusive praise and repeat it several times to pattern the correct behavior.

TRAINING EQUIPMENT

To begin your training, you'll need a 6-foot leather or nylon lead and a tight-fitting buckle collar. For your dog's safety and comfort, do not use a "choke collar" that tightens when you apply pressure on the lead. You may also want to have some food treats, a ball or a toy handy for extra incentives and rewards. When you progress to off-lead training, a 4-inch to 6-inch nylon or leather lead,

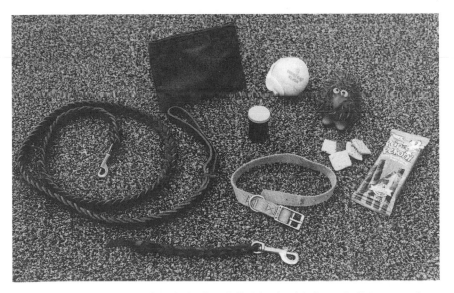

Agility training equipment (*clockwise from left*): 6-foot lead, bait pouch, film can, tennis ball with belt clip, dog toy, food treats, buckle collar, tab

called a tab, will be useful. The tab should be long enough to grab quickly but short enough so that it does not interfere with your dog's movement.

Another handy training device is an empty film can—a small plastic container designed to hold a roll of photographic film. Filled with delectable doggy treats, it can serve as a multipurpose motivator. A dog rewarded with food from the can will soon learn to "key" on it. The film can then makes a great target for teaching the dog to work ahead of you. To increase motivation you can throw the can over hurdles and on ahead when your dog exits the tunnels and weave poles. This is especially useful for dogs that are not toy- or ball-oriented. Although you could throw food without a film can, it is not a good idea because the food is often too small for the dog to see and thus encourages the dog to spend time sniffing the ground looking for food.

COMMANDS AND SIGNALS

The way you communicate to your dog which obstacle to perform is through a clear, consistent verbal command accompanied by a clearly visible signal. Why use both? Because you can! It's extra insurance. In certain situations your dog will respond best to a visual signal, and in others, to an audible command. A signal can save the day when it is so noisy that your dog won't hear your command, such as during a rainstorm under a metal-roofed building, while a plane is flying overhead or when a huge crowd is cheering you along. A signal can also make up for a late verbal command—something for which new trainers are famous, as are a few seasoned ones! Other times your dog will need to rely on your verbal command, for example, while working ahead of you. Also, using signals along with your commands during training teaches your dog to watch your hands. This will pay off when working on control between obstacles.

For each obstacle you will need to choose a command that you will use consistently to tell the dog to perform that particular obstacle. Some suggestions for commands are provided in my discussion of each obstacle, and are summarized at the end of this chapter. Generally speaking, you should choose a different command for each obstacle that appears visually unique from the dog's point of view, since your goal is to teach your dog to discriminate between certain obstacles by voice command alone.

Get in the habit of giving a command only once and then enforcing it. In the learning stages, "enforcing it" means gently helping the dog to begin performing the obstacle. If you become accustomed to repeating commands over and over, your dog will become desensitized and the command will cease to have meaning. It also teaches your dog that if the command is missed you're sure to repeat it. Giving one command also reinforces the element of teamwork between you and your dog. When performing in the ring, it demonstrates that you are a smooth-working team and that your dog fully understands who is the team leader.

The way you communicate to your dog which obstacle to perform is through a clear, consistent verbal command accompanied by a clearly visible hand signal.

Giving one command during your early training will pay off if you plan to go on to compete at advanced levels, where you are penalized for a significant hesitation in response to the command, called a refusal. If you and your dog are in the habit of giving/receiving multiple commands, the judge may decide that your dog refused your first command, even if you did not give enough time to respond before giving your second command.

The hand signals you use must be clearly visible to your dog to be effective. The best signals are clear, deliberate extensions of your arm, with your hand held flat and extended vertically. Many people use a pointed finger to direct their dogs—after all, we humans point a finger to indicate direction to another human! *Dogs don't see it that way.* From a distance a pointed finger is much more difficult to see than a flat hand. Try it yourself! Get down on your dog's level and have a friend signal you from a distance of 30 feet, first with a pointed finger and then with a flat hand. Which is easier to see? Competitive obedience exhibitors figured this out long ago—that's why you see flat hand signals used almost exclusively in the Obedience ring.

To be effective your signal must also be steady and deliberate. A momentary flash of a signal may not be noticeable to your dog, which could have been concentrating on jumping and not watching for your hand during that brief moment.

A dog's-eye view of hand signals—flat hand vs. pointed finger. Which is easier to see?

PACING YOUR TRAINING

Every dog is different. Your dog may learn an obstacle quickly while another dog needs more time. Some dogs get bored with frequent repetitions, and some are driven to perform again and again. If this is the first time you have "worked" with your dog, you will discover these things and more. To get the most out of your dog, determine what works best and adjust your training methods. At no time do you want your dog to become bored or overtired!

Learning something new is stressful, so follow your praise with brief sessions of play between exercises to relieve your dog (and you) of any tension. Always end your sessions on a successful note—perhaps with an exercise your dog especially enjoys. It's best to end your sessions with the dog wanting to do more, and not becoming overtired or bored. If your dog tires easily, check weight. Perhaps the dog could stand to lose a few pounds. If not, more physical exercise such as running or swimming may help improve stamina.

When training an obstacle, if you experience a problem or setback that the dog can't seem to overcome, make the exercise easier (for example, shorten the tunnel or lower the hurdle) to get one successful performance and then praise profusely and quit that particular exercise for the day. Take heart, for there comes a point when every dog says (or at least thinks), "Ah-ha! That's what

Learning can be stressful, so be sure to include frequent play sessions between exercises.

this is all about—No problem, Mom!'' This point comes at different times for different dogs, but it almost always comes.

Don't worry about speed in the early stages of training. I've had frustrated beginning students remark to me, "Bruno finally does the obstacle but he sure is slow!" Not to worry. (At least, not yet!) Speed comes with confidence, and confidence comes with practice and familiarity. The first time you typed a letter, you managed to crank it out, but how fast did you do it?

OBSTACLE TRAINING PROCEDURES—PIECE BY PIECE

Having dwelled long enough on "words of wisdom" to prepare you for your training, it's time to introduce your dog to each of the obstacles.

Pipe Tunnel

Many dogs consider the pipe tunnel their favorite obstacle (yes, we've taken a poll!). For this reason, and because it is relatively simple to master, the tunnel is a good obstacle with which to begin your training.

If you have one available, start your dog through a short barrel to convey the concept of a tunnel and to instill confidence at the start. The barrel can be

The pipe tunnel is a favorite among canines.

30

a cardboard or plastic industrial drum, or a large plastic garbage pail with the bottom cut out. We use the barrel from our collapsed tunnel since it is already mounted on a platform to prevent it from rolling, and it contains antislip material on the dog's walking surface. If you don't have a barrel available to you, you can use your pipe tunnel; however, shorten it to a length of about 2 to 3 feet by compressing it.

To begin your training, choose a command to use to direct your dog through the pipe tunnel. "Tunnel" and "Through" are popular choices. Using a 6-foot lead, place your dog in a lying down position as close to the barrel opening as possible. Have someone hold your dog still as you move to the other end of the barrel. Thread the lead through and hold it in your hand. Establish eye contact, use your command and encourage the dog to come to you through the barrel. If the dog struggles to get away from the tunnel opening, get extra help to hold the dog in position in front of the barrel and continue encouraging the dog to come through. After making several successful passes through the barrel, the dog will usually begin to enjoy the game. Now you can begin "run-bys."

With your dog on-lead at your left side, stand about eight feet from the barrel and focus your dog's attention on the opening. Take a running start at the barrel, signaling at the opening with your flat left hand, and give the command you have chosen for the tunnel. Drop the lead as your dog enters the barrel and run to the end and greet with lots of praise. If the dog is reluctant to enter, try

Teaching the barrel as an introduction to tunnels.

again, this time holding the lead as close as you can to the collar and waiting to release it until the dog's head is inside the barrel opening. Praise as the dog continues through the barrel. After two or three successful run-bys using the barrel, you are ready to advance to the actual pipe tunnel.

To begin to teach the tunnel, make sure that it is arranged in a straight line so that you will be able to establish eye contact with your dog, as you did when using the barrel. Use the same method to call your dog through. If the dog becomes panicky, compress the tunnel to a shortened length of about 4 feet long. At this length you can thread your lead all the way through the tunnel and use the lead to encourage your dog. When the dog is going through the tunnel confidently at this shortened length, gradually increase to the tunnel's full length.

After your dog has learned to do reliable "recalls" (calling the dog through the tunnel), begin run-bys by approaching the tunnel, commanding and signaling. Alternate working off your left (with your dog on your left side) with working off your right (with your dog on your right side), always signaling with the hand that is closest to the dog. When working on-lead, this will be the hand holding your lead, so it may be difficult to give a clear signal until you drop your lead. When the dog catches on to this "game," eliminate the lead and concentrate on clear signals. Be sure to give generous praise and encouragement as the dog exits the other end.

A word of caution: Don't be tempted to throw food or toys into the tunnel as a means of increasing speed or motivation. This encourages the dog to stop inside the tunnel and search for the toy or food. What can result is a dog that moves slowly through the tunnel or one that stops midway inside to sniff around.

We once had a Borzoi in a beginner class that was having trouble mustering the courage to enter the tunnel. The owner decided to throw a treat inside as a motivator. The dog reluctantly entered to get the treat, and after finding and eating it, found itself stopped inside this dark, scary tube. In a state of panic, the dog popped its head out through the top to escape! This traumatic experience destroyed the dog's confidence . . . not to mention the tunnel.

This illustrates the need to reward your dog only after he exits the tunnel. To increase speed and motivation, throw a ball, toy or a film can filled with treats *after the dog exits*, although not every time or the dog will learn to take off away from you after leaving the tunnel every time.

After your dog is happily doing run-bys through a straight tunnel at full length, bend it slightly so that some light is still visible to the dog through the tunnel. When confident with a slight bend, gradually increase the severity of the bend until your dog can perform the tunnel at a run-by when it is formed in a U shape.

Next, work on sending your dog ahead of you through the tunnel. Start by sending from only a few feet and gradually increase the distance until your dog is reliable when sent to the tunnel on one signal and command from a distance of 30 feet.

If at any point the dog shows reluctance, shorten your distance and try

Throwing a ball as your dog exits the tunnel can help increase speed and enthusiasm.

again. Most dogs will learn faster if you show them that you are placing a toy or treat at the other end of the tunnel. However, unless you are using food in a container (such as a film can), have an assistant stand on the other side of the tunnel to pick up the toy or treat should your dog try to run around instead of through the tunnel. It's important to prevent rewarding for incorrect behavior. The next time, block the dog's path so that the tunnel must be negotiated to get the reward.

When you can send your dog reliably to the tunnel while standing 30 feet in front of it, try sending from the same distance but at an angle so that the dog must work harder to approach the tunnel opening.

Collapsed Tunnel

Because the collapsed tunnel is more challenging than the pipe tunnel, introduce the collapsed tunnel only after your dog is confident performing the pipe tunnel.

The command you use can be the same as the one you use for the pipe tunnel, or you can select a different command, such as "Chute." To train the

Teaching the collapsed tunnel.

34

collapsed tunnel, begin by rolling back the chute so that the entire tunnel is only about four feet long. With a 6-foot lead, place your dog in a down position at the opening and have someone hold the dog in position. Thread your lead through the tunnel, go to the end and hold open the chute so that the opening is as large as the tunnel entrance. Establish eye contact and call the dog through using the command you have chosen. Praise, play and repeat.

When the dog is confident, try a run-by with an assistant holding the chute open from the side so that the assistant is not visible to the dog through the tunnel opening. With your dog on-lead, stand about 15 feet from the tunnel opening. With excitement and enthusiasm, focus your dog's attention on the tunnel and run toward it, giving your command and signal. If your dog is reluctant, gently guide him by the collar through the opening, praising when the dog has committed to entering the tunnel. If still met with reluctance, go back to the recall.

If the run-by is successful, have your assistant gradually increase the length of the chute in increments of 2 to 4 feet while still holding the end wide open so that a complete circle of light is clearly visible to the dog. Most dogs catch on to this very quickly, since you have already trained the pipe tunnel.

After doing successful run-bys using the full length of the chute, begin lowering the chute after the dog enters the tunnel so that it rests on your dog's back as the dog runs through. Gradually lower the top of the chute closer to the ground until the dog is pushing through the entire chute. Then alternate working off your left and right sides.

Always be sure that the chute is untangled and smooth before sending your dog through the collapsed tunnel. If Phideaux becomes tangled, it could damage the dog's confidence. If your dog does manage to become tangled, assist in finding the opening quickly but without making a fuss; then repeat the obstacle immediately, making it easier by rolling up the chute and holding it open. It is important that the dog be successful right away to restore confidence.

When the collapsed tunnel has been mastered with you running alongside, begin sending your dog through the obstacle from a distance, using the same method described for the pipe tunnel. This is more difficult than it may seem since some dogs can sense where you are and may try to head in your direction. As a result, the dog may turn around halfway through the tunnel and get tangled in the chute. You can overcome this tendency by placing food or a toy a foot or two from the exit of the chute and letting your dog know it's there. Be careful not to give verbal encouragement from your direction once the dog has entered the chute. This may be confusing and cause the dog to turn around in the chute to follow the sound of your voice. If the dog needs verbal encouragement, have a friend cheer from the exiting end.

As soon as the dog is confident working off either side of you on one command and at a distance, begin introducing the concept of a *wet* collapsed tunnel. Some dogs don't mind getting wet at all, while some would rather avoid it. Don't wait to find out how your dog reacts until the day you enter a rainy outdoor competition—simulate damp conditions during practice! Start by lightly misting the chute with a spray bottle, then gradually progress to a soaking wet chute. The wetter the chute, the harder your dog has to push to get through. Small dogs sometimes need extra encouragement. If your dog refuses to go through a damp or wet tunnel, back up in your training by rolling back the chute to a workable length and threading your lead through, progressing to holding the chute open for run-bys, etc. Provide your dog with a special reward for bravely overcoming this aversion.

Weave Poles

The weave poles are the most difficult obstacle for most dogs to perfect, even though they may look innocuous when sitting next to the imposing dog walk or A-frame. Other obstacles, such as the tunnels and hurdles, are naturally exciting to many dogs. When they play, you often see them burrow under coffee tables or leap over obstacles in their path. However, at no time does a dog naturally see a set of upright poles and decide to serpentine through them—it's an action that you must train.

There are almost as many techniques for training the weave poles as there are trainers—and all enjoy a degree of success. Many British trainers advocate methods that focus on speed first, then gradually introduce the dog to performing the weaving motion. The benefits of these methods are that the dogs have an immediate, pleasant experience with the weave poles and the handlers don't have to work hard to maintain the dogs' enthusiasm and speed. The disadvantages are that these methods are more difficult to set up (often involving the stringing of wires), are more time-consuming (the dog takes longer to learn the obstacle) and require a greater knowledge on the handler's part about what to do when the dog has a problem with skipping poles or incorrect entry. It is easy for the dog to get confused and for the handler to become frustrated.

Our method is a more practical and conventional approach. Using this method, a novice trainer should not encounter any problems that are too difficult to correct without help. Granted, it *does* require effort on your part to maintain the dog's enthusiasm, but it also produces quicker results. Experience and motivation will eventually result in speeds that are competitive with dogs taught using British methods.

Before beginning to teach the weave poles, decide what command you will use. "Weave," "Poles" and "Snake" are all good choices. You sometimes hear handlers use a two-word command such as "In-Out" each time the dog is supposed to weave in and out of the poles. This is a poor choice for many reasons:

- You may get confused and tell your dog "Out" when you want it to go "in."
- You eventually want the dog to sail through the poles faster than you will be able to say "In-Out-In-Out-In-Out."

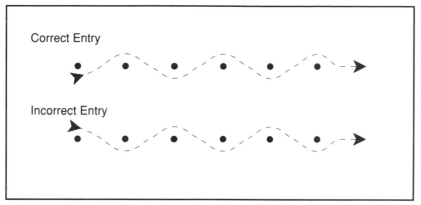

Correct Entry

Incorrect Entry

The dog must enter the weave poles to the right of the first pole.

- You eventually want to be able to call the dog and send the dog through without you, and it will be difficult for you to command each pole from a distance.
- You eventually want to handle off your right side as well as your left. What, then, constitutes "in"?

Standing in front of and slightly to the right of the weave poles, position your dog on-lead at your left side. Bunch up the lead in your left hand as close to the dog's collar as possible, and place your right hand at the dog's eye level so that the dog can follow your hand through the poles. As specified in the *Official Rules and Regulations of the United States Dog Agility Association*, your dog must enter to the right of the first pole and must continue weaving in and out without skipping a pole.

Excite the dog, focus attention on your hand and give the command that you have chosen. Step in close to the poles with your left leg to cue the dog when to weave away from you, and then move to your right when you want to cue to come back to you. Some people achieve excellent results by swinging their hips from left to right "hula style" as an added cue to the dog. This may feel a bit ridiculous at first, but take solace in that once your dog learns how to weave, physical cues from you will no longer be required.

If the dog is distracted or bored when weaving, as indicated by looking everywhere but straight ahead or at your hand, place an incentive in your right hand, such as a food treat, ball or toy. Give the dog the reward only after successful weaving through all the poles.

Teaching the weave poles takes frequent repetition—and that's where the dilemma exists. Because it's not naturally fun for the dog to weave, you need to go out of your way to make it exciting, which means frequent, short training sessions with extra motivation. To maintain enthusiasm use your voice to create excitement before working the poles. Possible words of encouragement include "Are you ready?" or "Do you want to?" Occasional inducement and reward

Teaching the weave poles—holding the lead close to the collar with the left hand while keeping the dog's attention with the right.

with food and/or toys can also help maintain your dog's interest. Three to five times through the poles several times a day should help get the idea across without overwhelming or boring your dog. Because of the repetition that is necessary, it pays to construct your own set of weave poles rather than relying on practicing only at class or during group work sessions. Appendix A on Obstacle Construction provides ideas for building various types of weave poles. The two major types are weave poles you drive into the ground and "freestanding" sets of poles that are permanently attached to a base.

If you are using individual poles that are driven into the ground, start with the poles positioned about 30 inches apart and slightly offset in a zig-zag pattern; then move them closer together and toward the center as the dog learns the exercise. Most of the weave poles you will encounter in competition are spaced at 20-inch intervals. If you have a medium or small dog, you may find it easier to use poles that are only 2 feet long when you start out. With shorter poles it is easier to work on-lead, since the lead isn't as likely to catch on the top of the poles and you will have more control holding the lead closer to the collar.

For a slightly larger investment in time and money you can construct a freestanding set of weave poles. If you're like most people, you'll practice more often if the poles are set up in your house. You won't have to worry about the weather or darkness. For our classes we have two sets of freestanding weave

Using short, frequent practice sessions and ample motivation, you can teach your dog to be fast, accurate and enthusiastic about the weave poles.

poles—a "regulation" set, built to competitive specifications, and a beginner set with shorter poles that are offset in a zig-zag pattern.

A terrific place to set up weave poles is in your living room or wherever you settle in to watch TV. The break during commercials is just about the right amount of time to spend practicing weave poles. Before long, your dog will be sitting by your side, waiting for the next set of commercials, eager to be your center of attention for the "weaving" game. Besides, it's healthier than taking a trip to the refrigerator.

When first teaching the poles, it is important not to rush. If your dog is truly working, allow work at any speed. However, do not allow distraction and stopping. When your dog negotiates the weave poles off-lead without physical cues from you, begin getting ahead to help increase speed, gradually increasing your distance. Stay close enough at first so that you can correct mistakes before they happen. Eventually you should be able to put your dog on a sit-stay at one end of the set of poles, go to the other end and call the dog through without his missing a pole.

Once your dog understands the mechanics of weaving through the poles, increase speed by clapping and cheering while the dog negotiates the poles. Throw a ball or toy after your dog correctly exits the last pole. Only reward accurate, quick performance. Your standard for "quick" can be increasingly

The "beginner" weave poles are slightly offset to make it easier for the dog to weave. The poles are shorter to allow the handler to hold the lead close to the collar. This is especially helpful when training small dogs.

more demanding as the dog catches on to what is expected. Eventually the dog will understand that you want both fast and accurate performance.

Once your dog has mastered the weave poles when approaching them from an optimal entrance angle (head-on and slightly to the right of the first pole), it is time to practice approaching from more difficult angles. Gradually change your approach angle until your dog can approach from the left side of the poles and still enter correctly from the right. It also pays to practice approaching from the right at a sharp 90-degree angle.

Training for High-Level Competition

If you are training your dog to compete at the highest levels, you will need to train your dog to weave off your right as well as your left. This will give you added flexibility in how you handle your dog and can result in faster times on the course. With weave poles, unlike other obstacles, you should wait until your dog is rock-steady off your left before starting to weave off your right. To begin your training, approach the poles in your usual manner, allowing the dog to get somewhat ahead of you, if possible. As the dog approaches the second pole, you quickly step around behind to the other side while the dog is weaving. The

Calling the dog through the weave poles.

momentum will usually carry the dog through without difficulty. If there is a momentary lapse, use your hand to give direction through the correct poles until the dog is going fast enough to be weaving on "auto-pilot" again. When you are successful, begin your approach with the dog working on your right. You may need to use a lead or a tab to get started from the correct side. As with anything having to do with weave poles, success comes through frequent, motivational repetition.

The next stage in training to be a super competitor is to begin sending your dog through the weave poles ahead of you. This maneuver can come in handy in Gamblers competition, or whenever you can save time by sending the dog ahead of you. Use only one set of five or six poles to begin with. Begin by approaching the poles in your normal manner, but hang back a bit. If the dog hesitates and looks back at you, meet up again and encourage the dog on. It sometimes helps to have a friend call your dog through as you are hanging back. If training alone, use your film can as your "assistant." Show your dog that you are placing the film can a few feet past the last weave pole. If the dog goes on ahead of you and weaves correctly, open the can and give a treat. A short cut to the film can (almost all dogs do this at first!) does not earn a treat. Instead, go back to the beginning and insist on his weaving correctly. It may take a bit of repetition, but the dog will eventually understand what you want. Once the dog is weaving ahead of you, you can discontinue using your film can as an incentive and instead provide intermittent reinforcement by throwing a ball, toy or your film can as the poles are exited after correct weaving.

Pause Table

Most dogs enjoy jumping on the pause table—perhaps they see it as being allowed to jump on furniture! The rules specify a 36-inch by 36-inch tabletop with a height no greater than the dog's "jump height" (the height your dog will be required to jump in competition). Your dog may not always have to perform the table at maximum height, so it's best to prepare for any situation by practicing on tables of different heights—ranging from 12 inches to your dog's maximum jump height.

Choose a command that is unique to the pause table. Most people use "Table." Do not use the same command you use to tell your dog to jump—if you do, you are asking for a jump over the table! Likewise, do not use the same command you use for any of the other obstacles.

Start with the dog on-lead, get the dog's attention and interest, use your chosen command and run with the dog to the table. Encourage jumping up by tapping the top of the table with your hand or by placing a toy or treat on the table. When the dog has four feet on the table, *praise immediately*.

Teaching the pause table.

Sending the dog to the pause table by placing a treat on the far side.

After learning to jump on the table, your dog must learn to lie down on it. If the dog has already been taught to lie down on command, simply give your command. Otherwise, encourage the down position using food or toys, or by gently walking the feet into a down position while simultaneously giving the down command. Praise as soon as the dog is completely lying down.

Now you must teach the dog to stay on the table in a down position. If you have already taught the down-stay, give your command. Otherwise, give a stay command and be prepared to hold your dog down should it try to get up. After a few seconds, release your dog using your release word and praise extensively. Gradually extend the length of time you expect your dog to stay to ten seconds or longer then give a stay command while you walk away, starting with short distances and working up to 20 feet.

It is to your advantage to use a hand signal and a verbal down command simultaneously. The signal is an extra cue to the dog and is perfectly legal, so why not use every advantage? The signal most people use for the command to lie down is a straight up and down motion with the right hand. In practice, if your dog does not go down immediately when commanded, use your signal hand for a downswing tap on the head or shoulders to get your point across. In competition, of course, you may never touch your dog.

As soon as your dog jumps on the pause table, give a simultaneous verbal command and hand signal to down.

It pays to practice a fast, reliable drop as a compulsive Obedience command, apart from the time and place you practice Agility. Some exercises to help you achieve speedier drops are described in chapter 4, Obedience Work.

Some dogs may be reluctant to jump onto the table. For these dogs, try starting with a lower table, if available. If not, try kneeling or standing on the table yourself while encouraging the dog to join you. You can also try showing your dog a treat or toy, placing it on the far side of the table, and have the two of you run to the table. Make sure that the dog doesn't go around to the back side to get a reward without jumping on the table! You might enlist the help of an assistant to prevent cheating, or use your film can (your "assistant in a can"!).

Another technique that can motivate your dog is to have an assistant restrain the dog about 10 feet from the table. Go to the other side of the table and begin enthusiastically cheering and encouraging your dog. After a few seconds, have the assistant release the dog, which, you hope, will charge toward you and jump on the table. These "restrained recalls" help increase the dog's motivation to move quickly—they work well for hurdles and tunnels as well!

When practicing the pause table, vary the amount of time you keep the

Using the "restrained recall" to encourage the dog to jump on the pause table.

dog in a down position—sometimes require a stay longer than five seconds to prevent the dog's anticipating your release. Practice with and without someone counting down, and practice with strangers milling around the table close to your dog while counting, as this will have to be endured in competition.

While you are training the obstacle on-lead, you can prevent certain bad habits from forming. *Never* let your dog slide off or jump off the table before assuming the down position. In competition this will cost you points and valuable time. Once you've had a perfectly flawless performance ruined by an exuberant slide off the table, you will realize how important this is.

When the dog is happy and comfortable performing the pause table, take the lead off and start sending the dog ahead of you to the table. Remember to use one clear command or signal. If the dog is reluctant to go without you, try putting a treat or toy on the far side of the table. Eventually eliminate the reward on the table and follow the dog out to reward. Gradually increase your distance until you can send the dog to the table from a distance of 30 feet on one command, from either your left or your right side.

After your dog shows confidence in running to the table from a distance, begin introducing the concept of downing on a table that has been dampened with water. In competition you are sure to encounter a damp or wet table from time to time. Make sure your dog has experienced a wet table in practice and knows what you expect. Start by lightly misting the table with a spray bottle and then gradually progress to a soaking wet table. If the dog refuses to lie down, gently but firmly insist, giving encouraging praise and perhaps a special reward while the dog is lying down on the wet table.

Pause Box

The pause box is similar to the pause table in that the dog must remain in the down position for five seconds inside the box. The handler must not step on or touch any part of the box.

This obstacle isn't used often since it is disliked by many handlers and judges. The main reasons for this sentiment are that judging tends to be subjective as to what constitutes "in" and "out" of the box, and that the appearance of the box can vary greatly from trial to trial. This makes it difficult to teach your dog to recognize and perform the pause box since it can appear different wherever you go. You may encounter a pause box constructed of PVC pipe of varying widths, wood, tape or four upright poles, although PVC is most commonly used. Another concern is that some handlers worry that poor "Phideaux" won't want to lie down on damp grass, or on the "smelly" dirt of a livestock arena. All of these concerns are valid, but since judges *do* use the pause box occasionally, it makes sense to train around these problems.

Fortunately, the pause box is easy and inexpensive to make and is simple to begin training indoors. You can construct a PVC pause box for just a few dollars: All you need are four lengths of PVC pipe and four corner elbow brackets to make a 4-foot square.

Begin training the obstacle on a clean, dry surface that is comfortable to your dog, such as carpeting, floor tile, concrete or dry grass. Choose a command that will be unique to the pause box. "Box" is a common choice. With your dog on-lead, focus attention on the box, give your command and walk with your dog to the box. As soon as the dog is completely inside the box, command and signal the down. *Remember, use only one command to down, then enforce, if necessary*. Release and praise when the dog is lying down completely. If the down is partially outside the box, quickly release and reposition the dog without allowing him to run out of the box first. After the dog has learned to down in the box, add the stay as you did for the pause table. Have your dog remain in the down position for at least five seconds while an assistant counts down and hovers around the box.

The rules allow for part of the dog to hang outside the box, but the amount that is acceptable is a subjective decision made by the judge. Because interpretations vary, train the obstacle so that none of the dog's legs or feet are ever allowed outside the box. If your dog is trained to this standard, then the judge will never have to make a judgment call. During practice, when your dog's front feet hang outside the box, gently press or tap on them with your foot to get your dog to tuck them in and praise quickly. Use a command such as "Tuck your

Teaching the pause box.

feet'' as you press on them. When you are in competition and Phideaux forgets to tuck his feet in, you can give a reminder command.

It's a good idea to practice with all allowable construction variations of the pause box, as well as combinations thereof, to prepare your dog for any type of equipment. When the dog understands the concept of ''box'' using PVC, use a box made from four 4-foot lines of duct tape attached to the floor or ground. When these are mastered, add four 4-foot poles to the corners of your taped box. Then try it with the poles only.

Practice on a variety of surfaces. In competition your dog may be asked to down on dirt, dry grass, wet grass, mud, pine needles, hay or a rubber mat. Any of these surfaces may contain scents that your dog may find offensive or attractive. After your dog has mastered the pause box on comfortable, familiar surfaces, progress to other surfaces, including damp and thoroughly wet ones. Agility trials are held regardless of weather, so it's best to be prepared for all conditions.

When your dog is proficient at performing different types of pause boxes under a variety of conditions, begin sending to an obstacle at a distance. Gradually increase your distance until the dog is going to the box reliably from a distance of 20 feet.

As you practice, move the location of the pause box frequently. Don't send your dog to the same spot every time. When I began teaching my first dog

Begin teaching the A-frame by flattening it to a height of 4 feet at the apex.

the pause box, I set up a PVC box in the house and began sending her across the room. After several sessions, she was racing to the pause box enthusiastically and assuming the down position, fully tucked in. Thinking to myself that we were making excellent progress, I then moved the box to the opposite side of the room. At the command "Box" she promptly ran to the same spot on the carpet she had been downing in all week—and she was so proud of herself! I had taught her to lie down in a specific place, not to look for the box! After that humbling experience, I moved the box each time I sent her.

A-Frame

To start dogs out, we lower our A-frame so that any dog can be successful without force. This requires a very sturdy A-frame and additional high-strength chain so that the apex of the A-frame is no more than 4 feet above the ground. At this shallow an angle, there is a great deal of force on the chain, so you may need to hammer stakes in the ground on both sides of the A-frame for additional support. Always test for sturdiness by walking over the A-frame yourself before asking a dog to perform the obstacle.

Choose a command that you will use for only the A-frame. Possible commands include "A-frame," "Scramble" and "Climb." With your dog on your left and on-lead, use your left hand to grip the lead about 10 inches above the collar. Focus the dog's attention on the A-frame, extend your left arm and take a running start, using the command you have chosen for the A-frame. Start with your left hand outstretched over the center of the ramp and move it as necessary to keep your dog on the ramp. At this very shallow angle most dogs enjoy walking over the obstacle. If your dog displays reluctance, encourage with food or toys, if necessary, but do not use a reward until the dog has reached the other side and is on the ground.

Keeping your dog on-lead, gradually increase the height over a period of several sessions until the apex of the A-frame reaches the full regulation height of 6 feet 3 inches. Be sure to use a head-on approach and give your dog enough room for a running start. Remain close by the side of the A-frame to prevent the dog from jumping off, and have a "spotter" positioned close to the other side.

As the A-frame becomes steeper, some dogs may reach a point where they become resistant to climbing the obstacle. If this occurs, your spotter can help encourage and/or lure the dog with a treat or toy, and if necessary, support the dog's rear to make the climb easier. When the dog reaches the top, allow Phideaux to look around and become acclimated to the height, then guide your dog down slowly. If the dog continues to resist after two or three "assisted" climbs, lower the A-frame a few inches to a height at which the dog feels confident. For persistently stubborn cases, check the dog's nails—if they are too long, climbing can be painful. End the session with a successful performance followed by abundant praise and play.

Another method for reluctant dogs is the "restrained recall," similar to that used for reluctance to jump on the pause table. Have an assistant hold the dog about 8 feet from the A-frame while the handler moves around to the opposite side of the obstacle and climbs up to the apex. The handler looks over the top of the A-frame while calling the dog enthusiastically. The assistant holds the dog for a few seconds, then releases the "spring-loaded" dog, which now has more incentive to climb.

As your dog becomes comfortable—and yes, wildly enthusiastic about performing the A-frame—most large dogs, some medium-sized dogs and a handful of small dogs will begin to miss the A-frame contact zones, especially on the way down. This is one of the biggest problems facing large-dog handlers.

As with any performance problem, do not let your dog miss contact zones repeatedly before you do something about it—to do so is to pattern the dog to make mistakes. Likewise, don't be satisfied with your dog barely touching the contact zones during practice. In the excitement of competition, your dog will be more likely to miss them. There are several ways to help alleviate contact zone problems, and one or more might be effective with your dog.

One approach is to position "contact zone hoops" at each end of the A-frame. The hoops are constructed of flexible plastic tubing formed in a circle

49

Two methods of training your dog to touch the A-frame contact zones: using contact zone hoops (*above*), and guiding your dog to the ground using food or a toy (*below*).

and fastened to a board. The dog must climb and descend the A-frame by passing through the hoops at each end. This pattern-trains the dog to touch the contact zones. The hoops are most effective if you use them *every time* the dog performs the A-frame once the dog becomes confident at full height. To introduce the hoops earlier in the training process complicates an already stressful learning situation. Different-sized hoops are needed for different-sized dogs. The hoop must be small enough to prevent the dog from missing the contact zone but large enough to allow him to pass safely through at a reasonable speed. For classes we keep several sizes on hand to accommodate all breeds.

Besides the hoops, there are many other techniques for handling contact zone problems. These include the following:

- **Hold a reward at the bottom of the down side every time the dog descends.** The dog should have to put muzzle to ground to receive the reward. Later, the motion of your hand toward the ground can be your signal to go all the way to the ground. At that point, you can use intermittent rewards to get a continued response to your signal.
- **Take off some of the antislip slats on the down side of the A-frame.** Your dog will learn to slow down and be careful when descending the A-frame. To prevent confidence problems, *don't remove the slats until the dog is performing the obstacle reliably and confidently.*
- **Practice the "Easy" command on-lead** (see chapter 4, Obedience Work). Large dogs can easily miss the contact zone on the up side if they approach the A-frame at too great a speed. The easy command is useful for controlling the dog's speed of approach, as well as the descent.
- **Teach your dog to wait at the top of the A-frame**, allowing you to get to the other side in order to control the descent.
- **Command your dog to down midway down the exit side of the A-frame**. In practice actually make the dog lie down, and reward in that position. Release and guide the dog down slowly, using the "Easy" command.
- When your dog reaches the apex, command "Easy," and when halfway through the descent, **place your right palm in front of the dog's chest to slow the descent while using your left palm to press the dog's shoulders downward toward the wall of the A-frame.** This helps communicate to your dog the crouching action you desire. After this has been learned, you can use your hands in similar positions, but not touching the dog, to signal a controlled descent.
- **Extend your arm in a straight line across the A-frame as a "bridge" your dog must duck under.** You can do this on both the up and the down sides of the obstacle. During practice, if the dog hits your arm due to an overly enthusiastic approach or descent, the dog will most likely modify the movement on the next try. This technique requires that you teach the dog to duck under your arm instead of jumping over

it, which is done by holding a barrier above your arm with your other hand. In competition you can use your arm as a signal, but you must be careful not to position your arm too close to the dog. If the dog hits you because you were too close or attempting to block movement, you will lose points.

When the dog is confident climbing the A-frame on your left, start alternating working off your left with working off your right until your dog is equally reliable working off either side.

Cross-Over and Dog Walk

Small dogs and puppies can be started on the cross-over or dog walk, but most larger dogs benefit from an introduction to ''plank'' obstacles by using a horizontal 2-inch by 10-inch plank raised about 12 inches off the ground. You can use cement blocks or sturdy plastic milk crates to support the plank. We use the plank from our see-saw since it is readily available and already equipped with a nonskid surface.

With your dog on your left, hold the collar in your right hand while placing

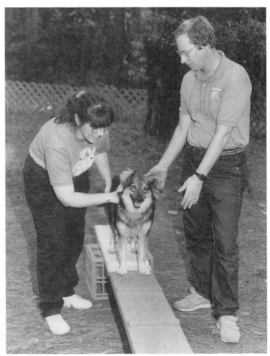

Teach your dog to walk a plank raised a foot above the ground before introducing the dog walk or cross-over.

your left hand near the dog's hip. Have an assistant remain close to the dog's other side. Approach the plank from a head-on position with friendly encouragement. Most dogs will walk the plank readily; however, for a dog that is reluctant, enlist the help of another assistant to lure the dog to the end of the plank with a treat or toy. If an enticement approach doesn't work, you may have to move each of the dog's feet to teach the security of step-by-step movement.

Some dogs will try to race across the plank—not out of confidence, but out of fear. When this happens, simply pull back on the collar and say "Easy," while you wrap your left arm around the dog and under the stomach to keep the dog on the plank. Repeat the plank walking until the dog is confident and surefooted without your holding the collar, and then proceed to the actual dog walk or cross-over obstacle.

If you have both a dog walk and a cross-over, begin training with the cross-over since it is less difficult for the dog to negotiate. Remove two of the planks so that the obstacle resembles a dog walk with a platform in the center. This configuration will allow you and a spotter to remain close to both sides of the dog at all times to prevent jumping or falling off the planks.

Choose a command that you will use for both the cross-over and the dog walk. These commands can be identical since the obstacles appear almost identical to the dog; but be sure to choose a command that you are not already using for some other purpose. Possible choices are "Dog Walk," "Walk On," "Plank" or "Up."

It is safest to teach this obstacle without your lead since the lead can dangle and get in the dog's way. Position your dog at your left side about 5 or 6 feet from the cross-over and in a direct line with the plank. Hold the collar in your right hand and place your left hand near the dog's right hip. Then give your command and guide your dog up the plank. Stay very close to the plank to prevent jumping off, while a spotter remains close to your dog on the opposite side. Hold back on the collar, if necessary, to maintain a slow pace. To steady the animal, place your left hand under the dog's stomach for support. You and your spotter must be prepared to prevent the dog from panicking and jumping off. *Never* let your dog fall or jump off the obstacle.

Some dogs have trouble getting their back feet on the board. For these dogs, make a chute using two boards and arrange them in a V to channel the dog onto the plank. Use the chute every time for this obstacle until the dog has learned where to place both back feet.

If the dog is reluctant to climb the plank after gentle encouragement, enlist the help of a third person to entice the dog with a treat or favorite toy. Occasionally, a dog will freeze and refuse to move regardless of the inducement. Here you may need to resort to moving each foot for the dog patiently, while continuing your encouraging words.

When your dog reaches the center platform, stop and allow him to get used to the height and recover from the ordeal. Praise and offer a treat. After about thirty seconds to a minute, begin the descent, maintaining a slow pace.

Using a V-shaped chute helps dogs learn where to place their back feet.

Some dogs may need several sessions of assisted plank climbs. If the dog does not seem to be improving, go back to the plank on the milk crates to renew confidence. When confidence returns on the plank, return to the cross-over, but this time begin by lifting and placing the dog on the down ramp, halfway down, and assist with the rest of the descent. Next, place the dog at the top of the down ramp. Then progress to halfway up the ramp. The dog should soon have the confidence to complete the entire obstacle without assistance.

Eventually the dog will realize that the cross-over is wonderful fun. When your dog is sure-footed and confident, try the obstacle without holding the dog's collar, but continue to provide spotters on both sides of the dog. If at any time your dog begins to bypass the plank by walking to the side of it, use a V chute or go back to holding the dog's collar. Bypassing should not be an option since in advanced classes it is considered a "refusal" and is faulted.

When your dog is happily performing the cross-over with two planks attached, it is time to add contact zone hoops (if you have chosen to use them)—similar to those used with the A-frame but narrower in width. The hoops help ensure that your dog continues all the way down the plank without taking a shortcut and missing the contact zone.

To continue your training, add the other two cross-over planks and begin making turns. The right turn is the easiest to master, thus it is a good one with which to begin your training. With your dog off-lead on your left, give the command to climb the plank. (By now the dog should be climbing the plank without you holding the collar.) When the dog is a few feet from the platform, command your dog to come and clap your hands to get the dog's attention.

Even if the come command is not yet known, the dog should respond to your clapping and encouragement. (You could also use the right and left commands if you have begun teaching them. These commands are described in chapter 4, Obedience Work.) If the dog is not responsive, gently grasp the collar and start guiding your dog down the correct plank. Always make sure your dog follows the plank all the way to the ground without jumping off.

Teach the left turn in a similar manner but with your dog on your right. If your dog is still reluctant to work off your right, as may be the case with some seasoned Obedience competition dogs, start with the dog on your left, and as all four of the dog's feet are "committed" to the plank, step around the end of the plank and switch to the other side.

When your dog is proficient in making both types of turns, you can begin teaching the dog to go straight across—which is by far the most difficult maneuver on the cross-over. Start by commanding the dog up one of the planks, and when he reaches the platform, give the command to down. If the down command is not yet known, guide the dog into a down position on the platform. The dog may need a sitting position first, and then you can either walk the feet down or lure the dog down with a treat. If moving quickly, your dog may need the down command before getting to the top to give it a moment to register. As soon as the dog is completely lying down, praise and command to stay.

If your dog is not steady on the down-stay, have an assistant hold him for you as you either duck under the plank or run around to the other side. (Either action requires caution on your part. If you decide to duck under, be careful not to hit your back or head on the underside of the plank—besides its being painful, you will lose points for touching the obstacle if you do this in competition. If you run around, be careful not to step on or trip over the plank in your path—this also qualifies as a point deduction.) When you reach the other side of the plank, release your dog from the stay and give guidance down the plank, making sure the descent continues all the way to the ground. Follow the exercise with exuberant praise and play.

When downing your dog on the platform, be sure to enforce the down command if there is no response on the first command—even if you were able to get to the other side without the dog continuing down the plank, insist on a down, or the dog will soon learn that you don't really mean what you say.

Once your dog is confident on the cross-over, you need to choose a handling method that suits your goals and preferences for the "straight across" option. The best method of handling the straight-across on the cross-over is to send your dog up the plank while you continue to move toward the other side. While you are moving, command your dog to down from a distance. Then release from

Using hoops helps pattern the dog to touch the contact zones on the dog walk and cross-over. For the best results, use different-sized hoops for different-sized dogs.

An elegant method of performing the straight-across on the cross-over: The handler sends the dog up the plank while continuing around the side, commanding and signaling the down from a distance.

that distance when you are on the other side of the obstacle and in a position to handle the contact zone. This can be quite fluid and fast, but it requires that your dog be confident and respond to your down command reliably at a distance.

An even more elegant but much riskier method is to send your dog straight across while you move to the next obstacle. It is relatively easy to teach the dog to continue straight across without you using the go-out command (described in chapter 4, Obedience Work). It is quite another matter to get the dog to touch the contact zone on the end of the exit plank consistently. Usually the dog turns to look for the handler while exiting off the side of the plank. You can try to teach your dog to touch the contact zone by putting food at the base of the opposite plank, with your contact zone hoops in place. The dog gets the reward only if it continues down the plank without you and exits through the hoop. You will need an assistant to remove the reward if the dog goes around the hoop, or you can use food enclosed in a film can.

Contact zones become more of a problem the more comfortable the dog becomes on the obstacle, although if you have been using contact zone hoops throughout your training, your problems will be minimized. Most of the techniques described for handling A-frame contact zones also apply to the plank obstacles.

Training the dog walk is usually a simple matter once the dog has mastered the cross-over. A few dogs display initial reluctance to walk the 12-foot horizontal

The dog walk is especially challenging for large dogs because of its narrow 12-foot horizontal plank.

plank, but overcome their fears with repetition, patience and encouragement. Use the same methods as you use for the cross-over, with spotters on both sides of the plank at all times. If the dog is not making progress on the dog walk, return to the plank on crates. When the dog is comfortable on the plank, return to the dog walk, placing the dog on the down ramp as described for the cross-over.

A few dogs in every group would benefit from a lower version of the dog walk as an intermediate step between the plank and the actual dog walk. If your budget and training area dimensions permit, you can build a lower version of the dog walk for training purposes. If not, when the time comes to build a new dog walk, you can modify your old one to suit this purpose.

See-Saw

To your dog, the see-saw is a dog walk that moves, so before attempting the see-saw, wait until your dog is comfortably performing the dog walk or cross-over. The addition of movement to climbing the plank can be unsettling for some dogs.

Choose a command that will be unique to the see-saw. ''See-Saw'' and ''Teeter'' are common choices. Always approach the see-saw from head-on, using the same technique with the see-saw as you used with the cross-over. With

Teaching the see-saw.

your dog on your left, remove your lead and hold the dog's collar in your right hand. Use your left hand to steady and catch the dog if it becomes necessary. Have a spotter remain close to the dog on the other side of the obstacle.

When your dog reaches the point where the see-saw starts to move, command "Wait" (or "Stay") and prevent the dog from proceeding. Have a second assistant gradually lower the board to the ground without letting it slam. Pause for a second, then allow the dog to continue down the plank at a controlled pace, *all the way* to the ground without jumping off. Respond with effusive praise and play.

Some dogs get panicky and attempt to jump off the see-saw, especially when it starts moving. If this occurs, place your arm around your dog with your left hand under the abdomen to support him and to prevent his jumping off. If extra encouragement is needed, enlist the help of a second assistant to entice the dog with a treat or toy.

As with the dog walk and cross-over, some dogs have trouble getting their back feet on the board. For these dogs, make a chute using two boards and arrange them in a V to channel the dog.

As the dog gains confidence on the see-saw (usually after two or three practice sessions), start allowing the board to rotate downward on its own. However, continue to stop the dog at the center and hold him there until well

The tire jump requires skill and precision on the part of the dog—especially with larger breeds.

after the rotation has stopped. This is extremely important to prevent the development of bad habits. In competition if your dog exits from the see-saw before the plank has touched the ground, major fault points are incurred for "fly-off." If you teach "Wait at the center," eventually the dog will learn to pause independently of you.

Tire Jump

The tire jump requires precision and confidence on the part of the dog—especially with larger breeds. The dog must jump precisely in the center, neither too high nor too low. The larger the dog, the more precise the performance must be. When training the tire jump, the key to steady improvement is to increase the tire's height *gradually, without becoming impatient.*

Before teaching the tire jump, choose your command. "Tire" is most often used. When choosing a command, avoid using the same command you use for jumping, otherwise your dog may try to jump over the top of the tire instead of through the middle!

To teach the obstacle, begin on-lead, with the tire height set so that your dog is almost stepping through but still has to hop. Put the dog in a sitting or standing position, close to and directly in front of the tire. Have someone hold your dog, or at least be ready to catch the dog if he tries to go around the tire.

Thread your lead through the tire and go around to the other side. Establish

Teaching the tire jump.

eye contact with your dog through the opening of the tire, and with a happy and excited expression, tap the inside bottom rim of the tire and give the command you have chosen. If the dog requires extra encouragement, show a food treat or a toy through the opening as an incentive. Be effusive with your praise as the dog jumps through the tire toward you. Repeat immediately at the same height.

Once your dog is reliable at performing recalls at a given tire height, progress to run-bys. On a shortened lead or tab, stand at least 8 feet away from the obstacle, approaching from head-on. Focus your dog's attention on the tire. Taking a running approach toward the obstacle, signal and give your command. Drop your tab as the dog begins to jump. Most dogs will jump through the tire readily. If the dog tries to squeeze between the tire and the frame, block the undesirable opening and try again. Clear acrylic plastic panels are ideal because the dog doesn't know there is a barrier.

During the early stages of training, it is best to perform the tire jump in only one direction during a training session. Jumping in the other direction presents a different background ''sight picture,'' which can complicate the learning process.

When your dog is performing run-bys smoothly at a given height, raise the tire an inch or two and begin again with recalls, progressing to run-bys.

Alternate working off your right with working off your left so your dog does not develop a preference for working off one side or the other. After finishing

Placing clear plastic panels under the tire prevents dogs from running underneath it.

each of your training sessions, remember the height at which the tire was set when you quit. When you start the next session, begin at this level (or an inch below) and continue to work upward.

Once you have trained your dog to perform the tire jump reliably at full height you should never lower the tire. The reason? You have gradually trained your dog to perform a precise and complex performance. Your dog can easily miscalculate the jump at the lower height and smash smartly into the top of the tire. The damage to your dog's confidence can be considerable.

Occasionally a dog will reach a jump height and prefer to go under the tire rather than jump through it. If this occurs, block the opening under the tire *every time you ask the dog to jump through it* until the dog appears to have caught on to what is expected.

Hurdles

Hurdles are more fundamental to your success in Agility than any other obstacles. Since they comprise a large percentage of the obstacles on a standard course, your dog will usually be required to jump some form of hurdle five to

Most Agility hurdles have decorative "wings"—a carryover from Agility's roots in equestrian events.

thirteen times in a single round. To be successful on the course, your dog must learn to jump smoothly and reliably while maintaining focus and enthusiasm.

Before beginning to teach the hurdles, decide what command or commands you will use. The simplest and perhaps the best solution is to select one command to use for all the hurdles. Popular choices are "Over," "Jump" and "Hup."

Some people feel that their dogs benefit from different commands for bar jumps, solid (board) jumps and long jumps, such as "Bar," "Hup" and "Over." (Where the bone jump and lattice jump fit in is anyone's guess!)

Some go so far as to assign each hurdle a different command, such as "Spread" and "Double." Feel free to choose this option—it may help your dog someday. But *you must be consistent*. Many handlers have enough trouble remembering the course and their planned strategies, while running at top speed and keeping one eye on their dogs. There's also the problem of unusual-looking hurdles. What do you do when you enter a trial and the hurdles look different from those you've practiced? How do you determine which commands to use?

Many of the more visually interesting Agility hurdles have "wings"—decorative side supports carried over from Agility's roots in equestrian events. It takes more confidence on the dog's part to jump hurdles with wings since the handler cannot run closely alongside the dog. It's best to begin teaching your dog using hurdles without wings since they are less likely to snag your lead and they allow you to remain closer to your dog. You can purchase ready-made portable hurdles without wings for training and practice from manufacturers of

You can purchase ready-made hurdles for training and practice from manufacturers of obedience training equipment. Pictured are an Obedience high jump, bar jump and broad jump.

obedience training equipment. An Obedience "high jump" (solid jump) and Obedience "bar jump" are adjustable in small increments and are available in lightweight plastic for portability.

Although the Obedience bar jump is suitable for use in competition, the high jump is not because the top board is usually not displaceable if a dog bumps into it. The Obedience "broad jump" is sufficiently similar to the Agility "long jump" to make it suitable for training and practice; however, you will need to add four corner pole markers to use it for competition. The corner pole markers are necessary so that the judge can determine if the dog has performed the jump without cutting any of the corners. To receive credit for performing the long jump, the dog must enter and exit between both sets of corner poles.

If you prefer to construct your own hurdles, you can copy the Obedience designs or be totally creative. One of our students taught her Corgi to jump in her kitchen using a dowel resting on two tuna cans, graduating to soup cans and then progressing to a combination of soup and tuna cans until she reached full jump height. Larger dogs may need a long hallway with a broomstick resting on two chairs or several paint cans. You can even use a leaf from your dining room table standing on end as a solid jump! Hallways are a great place to practice jumping since you can easily arrange it so that it is difficult or impossible for the dog to go around the hurdle.

Solid Jumps

It's best to start the dog with a solid jump rather than a bar jump since you can teach the dog the mechanics of jumping without the possibility of the dog deciding to go under the bar. Start with the hurdle set at your dog's elbow height. With your dog on-lead about 8 feet from the jump, focus attention ahead of you and give the command to jump. Run toward the obstacle and jump over it with your dog. Praise and repeat. Then progress to recalls: Put the dog in a sit-stay position (or have someone hold the collar), go to the other side, tap the top of the hurdle and give your command. Respond with exuberant praise and play when your dog complies!

For reluctant dogs, encourage with a toy or treat. Another motivational method is the "restrained recall," described earlier for the pause table, in which an assistant holds your dog facing the hurdle while you encourage a "frenzy of jumping excitement." The assistant then releases as your dog is straining to come to you.

If a dog remains reluctant to jump a very low hurdle, check for a physical problem. Examine paw pads for sores or burns. If there is no sign of injury, consult your veterinarian before continuing your training.

When your dog can do reliable recalls, progress to run-bys. Stay very close to the side of the hurdle to prevent your dog from going around it. For reluctant dogs, throw a ball, toy or film can filled with food over the hurdle as you approach it. Eventually throw it only as a reward after the dog has landed on the opposite side. Then use the reward only intermittently.

When your dog is happily doing run-bys on-lead, move on to off-lead work. Continued jumping on-lead can cause jump-technique and confidence problems, so it is best to move off-lead as soon as possible. Then gradually begin raising the jump height. Two inches per week is a good rule of thumb. As with all obstacles, practice running with your dog on your left as well as on your right.

When confident off-lead, begin using solid jumps with wings. Begin as you did with the solid jump by jumping along with your dog first, then doing recalls and finally progressing to run-bys. Resist the temptation to begin with run-bys—your dog has never seen a winged hurdle before. You don't want the dog to jump over the wing!

For dogs that bypass the hurdles, keep them set at a very low height and work on-lead with motivational techniques until the dog is jumping reliably. Frequent, short practice sessions will help you get your point across without "burning out" the reluctant dog.

Bar Jumps

Teach the bar jumps using the same method you use for the solid jumps. The only added twist is that your dog may, at some point, discover that it is possible to go under the jump. This is good! You want this to occur in practice

Possible remedies for dogs that "walk" the long jump: Turn boards on their sides (*top*), place a bar on top of one of the boards (*middle*), position a bar jump over the long jump, set at a low height (*bottom*).

so that your dog learns that diving under the bar is unacceptable. There are many ways you can convey this to the dog. The first one to try is to lower the hurdle immediately to a height your dog is unlikely to go under, tap the bar and give encouragement to jump. Then very gradually increase the height, making it clear you are extremely pleased with each jump. If and when the dog decides to go under, go back to the original side of the hurdle without delay. Encourage enthusiastically and command to jump. If the dog continues to go under, try one of the following:

- Place a sheet of clear acrylic plastic as a barrier under the bar.
- Attach taut strands of nylon string in an X shape under the bar.
- Hang clear plastic sheeting over the bar, allowing it to dangle to the ground.
- Place an object, such as a mound of chicken wire, that is unpleasant to walk on directly underneath the bar.

Another problem some dogs develop with bar jumps is the tendency to bump or "tick" the bars, sometimes displacing them. If you notice your dog ticking a hurdle more than once during a practice session, even if not knocking off the bar, you have identified a problem that needs correcting. To correct a bad habit of "ticking" the hurdles, try either of the following suggestions:

- Affix a strip of clear acrylic plastic or taut nylon string about 1 or 2 inches above the bar. The dog will (one hopes) graze the string or plastic and learn to jump the hurdle by allowing a greater clearance than before.
- Weigh down the uppermost bar by filling it with sand and taping the sides closed. The dog will feel a correction as its toes graze the top of the bar.

It is easiest to teach the "spread-type" hurdles such as the double-bar and spread-bar jumps using several single-bar jumps that you can position with any spacing you desire. Use the same progression of steps you use with the single-type jumps, starting at first with the bars set at a low height and placed as closely together as possible. As the dog gains confidence, gradually increase the amount of height and spread until you reach your dog's full height.

Long Jumps

Teach the long jump using the same method as the other hurdles. Begin by jumping with your dog, progressing to recalls, then run-bys and then off-lead run-bys, gradually increasing the width of the spread. A problem many people encounter when their dogs are first introduced to the long jump is that the dogs want to walk across the boards rather than jump over them. To the dog the long jump may look like a contact obstacle!

The first time a dog "walks" the long jump or broad jump, take steps to prevent it from happening again. Here are some suggestions:

- Remove one or two boards and spread the remaining ones farther apart. When the boards are pushed together, the long jump can appear to the dog to be a contact obstacle. By removing some of the boards, you make it more difficult for the dog to walk across.
- Turn some or all of the boards on their sides, making it difficult or impossible to walk over. Gradually turn each of the boards upright until the dog is jumping the entire obstacle.
- Place a striped bar on top of one of the long jump boards. This may be enough to let the dog know you expect a jump. Or place bar jump stands on either side of the jump and lay a striped bar across at a height a few inches above the board.
- Lay a piece of chicken wire (with sharp ends turned under) over the boards.

Miscellaneous Hurdles

Some hurdles don't fit neatly into categories of solid, bar or long jumps. The bone jump and the lattice jump are two examples. You can begin teaching

When training any new type of hurdle, such as this "bone jump," begin with recalls with the hurdle set at a low height.

Turn familiar hurdles into strange-looking ones by "disguising" them periodically.

miscellaneous hurdles such as these after your dog is jumping solid and bar jumps reliably. When training any new type of hurdle, begin with recalls at a low height before progressing to run-bys.

Training organizations are permitted to construct jumps to take on almost any appearance—some may even frighten your dog—so you would be wise to practice on as wide a variety of strange-looking hurdles as possible. You can create all sorts of weird-looking hurdles during your practice sessions using white-elephant items from your garage and your imagination. Here are a few suggestions:

- Hang coats, hats and scarves on hurdles.
- Criss-cross bars from your bar jump or place them on a diagonal (this is done occasionally in competition!).
- Drape inflatable snakes, feather boas or Christmas stockings over the hurdle.
- Attach foliage to and around the jumps using cut branches and potted plants. (A common miscellaneous hurdle is a "brush jump"—a double bar jump with foliage or hay positioned between the bars.)

SUMMARY

Once your dog is performing all of the obstacles flawlessly, don't stop your training there. Move the obstacles to new locations within your training

69

area or, better yet, to entirely new areas. It may seem strange to humans, but changing the direction in which your dog performs an obstacle or shifting its position by only a few feet can make it appear completely new and different to your dog. The angle at which the light hits the obstacle and the background the dog sees while approaching it both contribute to a "sight picture" the dog associates with that obstacle. If you move your equipment regularly, your dog will become acclimated to a wide variety of sight pictures and will be more competitive in the Agility ring.

As you continue with your training, keep in mind some of the important points from this chapter.

For your dog's safety:

- Use a flat buckle collar (or no collar at all) when training Agility—not a "choke" or slip collar.
- When training the contact obstacles, always use a spotter to prevent your dog from jumping or falling from an obstacle.
- Once you have reached full height on the tire jump, don't practice it at a lower height.
- Always make sure the collapsed tunnel chute is smooth and straight before sending your dog through it.

To get the most out of your dog's performance:

- Don't sour your dog with overwork or harsh discipline. Remember that Agility is for fun, so be generous with your praise.
- Always end your sessions on a successful note.
- Teach your dog to work off both your right side and your left side from the very start.
- Don't allow your dog to repeat the same mistake several times. To do so is to pattern the wrong behavior.
- Incorporate periods of play between exercises to alleviate stress and to keep learning fun.
- Choose a command for each obstacle and consistently use it in your training. A summary of suggestions for commands appears below:

Tunnels	"Tunnel," "Through," "Chute" (if desired, for collapsed tunnel)
Weave Poles	"Weave," "Poles," "Snake"
Pause Table	"Table"
Pause Box	"Box"
A-Frame	"Scramble," "Climb," "A-Frame"
Dog Walk and Cross-Over	"Dog Walk," "Walk On," "Plank," "Up"
See-Saw	"See-Saw," "Teeter"
Tire Jump	"Tire"
Hurdles	"Over," "Jump," "Hup"

4

Obedience Work

ANYONE WHO has endured the antics of a dog with no manners understands the value of an obedience-trained dog. Having a few basic Obedience commands at your disposal, such as "Sit," "Stay," "Down" and "Come," gives you the power to communicate your wishes in a language both you and your dog understand. This translates to a strengthened relationship, a happier pet and a livable household environment.

Obedience training can give your dog a fuller life, since a dog that is well-behaved and under control can visit the homes of friends, attend outdoor festivals and share more of your activities with you. It can also lengthen the dog's life. Consider the situation in which your dog slips by you as you open the front door, sees a squirrel and runs into the road as a car is coming. If your dog has been trained to come or down without hesitation despite distractions, you have a lifesaving tool. As an added bonus, you also have a tool you need to advance in your Agility training.

HOW MUCH OBEDIENCE TRAINING IS NECESSARY?

To teach your dog the individual obstacles, no previous obedience training is required; to teach your dog to run with you without a leash ("off-lead") and perform specific obstacles in sequence at your command, your dog must have some basic obedience training—specifically, reliable responses to the sit, stay, down and come commands. Knowing how to heel at your left side is also helpful, but not required. By far the most critical obedience requirement for off-lead

Obedience-trained dogs can go anywhere.   *Photo: Gordon Simmons-Moake*

sequencing is a reliable response to the come command. Ideally, your dog should come on your first command, regardless of the distractions present. (Even if a child is dangling an ice cream cone in front of your dog's nose!)

Dogs that have earned advanced Obedience titles such as Companion Dog Excellent or Utility Dog can usually learn to be competitive faster than those without advanced training. These dogs are accustomed to working in Obedience rings and have been taught to ignore distractions, already jump full height on command and may have begun signal work. Also, the handlers are more familiar with training techniques and the timing of corrections and praise, and have already established a working rapport with their dogs. On the other hand, those without Obedience backgrounds often have enthusiastic dogs that are happy to get out of the house and do something fun with their owners. I've seen some top Agility competitors come from the ranks of pet owners who never took a formal obedience class in their lives.

To continue your training past the individual obstacle level, you need *reliable* responses to the sit, stay, down and come commands. "Heel," "Easy," "Go-Out" and "Right" or "Left" are other useful commands that can help you in many situations but are by no means essential. This chapter provides a sampling of techniques for training the Obedience commands used in Agility. It is in no way intended to be an all-inclusive obedience training guide. The

72

concepts are provided in a nutshell and don't include all the "whys" and "what-to-do-ifs." Many excellent books are totally devoted to the subject and are invaluable resources for those seeking additional detail or alternative methods for obedience problem solving. One of the best ways to work through obedience problems is to enroll in a training class with a knowledgeable instructor. Practicing Obedience commands around other dogs will have a positive effect on your Agility training.

In your Obedience work, adhering to a few key principles will help you maintain a fair and productive working relationship with your dog:

- When teaching a new Obedience exercise, try to obtain the desired behavior without using force. Often you can guide the dog into the proper position using food, toys or encouragement. The dog will learn the exercise faster than if you "push" her into position and both of you will enjoy your training sessions more.
- Keep in mind that learning is stressful—inject frequent play sessions in your training to relieve tension.
- Give big rewards for big successes—and quit (for the day) while you're ahead.
- When teaching something new, reward for correct behavior regardless of how it occurred—be it by the dog's own intent, by accident or through assistance from you.
- With all Obedience work, be careful to *give your command only once*. If the dog does not obey, *enforce the command*. During the early learning stages, enforcing the command entails gently showing what you expect. In the latter stages of training, the type of enforcement you choose involves "reading" your dog.

If the dog is confused, give guidance. If you are convinced that your dog understands and is physically capable of obeying but has chosen not to, apply a correction. Corrections can range from a disapproving look, to a quick pop and release on the dog's lead, to a shaking and stare-down (the latter of which you may want to reserve for displays of aggression or urinating during an exercise). For minor infractions start small and use only as much correction as you need to prevent the dog from repeating a mistake. In some cases, to be effective, you may need to use a "training collar" such as a slip chain. Unless you are already skilled at administering safe, fair corrections using a training collar, you'd be wise to enroll in an obedience class for guidance. Training collars should be reserved for Obedience work, not Agility training.

- A useful verbal correction is the "Anhhh!" command. Less personal than the command "No!," the *Anhhh!* sounds like a buzzer on a television quiz show. Use it to let the dog know this is a wrong choice and then help to make the right one.
- Remember that training is context-sensitive. For example, if you train

the down-stay only in your own yard without distractions, you cannot assume the dog understands a down-stay in a public place with distractions. Gradually move your training to new areas, including public places, treating each new situation as a new learning experience. Then "proof" the dog on knowledge of the commands by gradually adding deliberate distractions such as people, food, toys and other animals.

- Choose a "release word," such as "Okay" or "Free," that you will consistently use to release your dog from your commands. Your dog should obey your commands until you say your release word.
- To maintain your dog's enthusiasm for Agility, practice your Obedience commands away from the place you practice Agility.
- Remember to keep your obedience training fun for your dog whenever possible!

THE *SIT* COMMAND

In competition, you need the sit command if you would like to leave your dog behind the start line to gain a head start. In lieu of teaching the sit command, you may choose to stay behind the line with your dog and hold her until it is time to begin your run, but this limits your options for a competitive start. The sit command is even more useful in your training sessions since many sequences require you to position your dog on a sit-stay while you go to another part of the course.

The training method I prefer is a commonly used motivational approach using food (or a toy if you prefer). Because the method is purely motivational, you can start a seven-week-old puppy doing fast, enthusiastic sits.

In a room free of distractions get your dog in a standing position and hold a treat close briefly to get Star's attention. Command "Sit" while raising the treat overhead slowly until the dog naturally sits to keep balance. If the dog decides to back up instead of sitting, you may need to start next to a wall or use your foot or other hand to prevent backing up. If you still have difficulty, gently lower the rear into a sitting position. Praise and give the treat as soon as the dog sits. Gradually add distractions and increase the speed at which your hand moves over her head. Reward selectively for fast sits. Eventually you will be able to eliminate the food as an incentive, using it only as a random reward.

THE *DOWN* COMMAND

A fast response to the down command will save you precious seconds on the pause table and in the pause box. It can also help you halt your dog's forward progress, either when approaching an incorrect obstacle or when descending the A-frame at too fast a pace.

Teaching the sit command with food.

Some dogs aren't thrilled about having to lie down at your command. Downing is a submissive posture and it announces to the world who is the true leader of your team, something of which dominant dogs would rather not be reminded. After working out any down problems with dominance, you may find that the dog becomes much more cooperative and less likely to challenge you in other areas. This is the start of a positive working relationship!

Since signals are extra insurance in the Agility ring, it makes good sense to teach your dog the signal for down and to use it consistently *with* your verbal commands. This can be useful in noisy situations. During practice you can use your signaling hand to tap the dog on the head or shoulders for failure to comply with your command.

As with any Obedience exercise, start with maximum motivation and minimum force. To teach the down, start with your dog in a sitting position. Show a piece of food and slowly bring it toward the floor while holding back gently on the collar to prevent moving forward. Command "Down" as you lower the food. The nose will follow the food and the dog will soon be lying down. Give the food and praise as soon as the dog is completely down. You

Teaching the down command with food.

may need to place your foot or other hand behind the rear to prevent backing up or lifting the rear as the front goes down.

You can remove your hand from the collar and can move the food toward the ground more quickly once your dog catches on to the game. When Phideaux is proficient at dropping quickly with food in your right hand, switch the food to your left and raise your right hand in a down signal (as you did while teaching your dog to perform the pause table) while lowering the food.

For dogs that are reluctant to lie down, make sure the treat is something the dog really wants, and practice while the dog is hungry. If food still doesn't motivate, use a favorite toy. Make every effort to keep this a fun and profitable game for your dog, but if motivation doesn't work, you must still insist on the down. Have patience and gently walk the dog's feet out at first. If there is no improvement after several repetitions, apply a swift downward pop on the collar to position Star down. Always follow with praise! Once your dog will lie down consistently from a sitting position without help from you, repeat the progression starting from a stand.

When your dog shows confidence in this exercise, use a game of "Random Drops." On-lead, excite your dog and run around in unpredictable directions. Without warning, command and signal your dog to down. If a drop is not immediate, apply a swift hand or leash correction. Make the dog stay in the down position for several seconds, exuberantly release, praise, excite and repeat.

If you have more than one dog at home, you can make fast drops into a

Playing "Mom says" around the house is a fun game that encourages fast responses to obedience commands.
Photo: Gordon Simmons-Moake

fun, competitive game. The game is similar to "Simon says." Around our household we call it "Mom Says" or "Dad Says" depending on who is playing the game.

To play, get a supply of wonderfully desirable, bite-sized food treats and let the dogs know what you have. Start walking around the house or yard nonchalantly, allowing the dogs to follow you around à la the Pied Piper. Without warning, turn around and give a signal and simultaneous command to down. The first dog down gets a treat. Release. Continue your strolling and try again. Soon, they should all get the hang of the game. Then change your command to another the dogs all know, such as sit, stand or speak. The fun is in keeping the dogs guessing. This game teaches the dog that it is enjoyable and rewarding to be attentive and to respond quickly to whatever command is given.

THE *STAY* COMMAND

Once your dog knows sit and down, you can add the stay command. In Agility, the stay is useful for leaving your dog behind the start line and for keeping your dog on the pause table or in the pause box for the full five seconds.

With your dog on your left side, command it to the desired position (sit or down). Then command and signal to stay (without using a name). To make the stay signal, swing your left palm from the left side of your body in front of the dog's nose without touching it. Step directly in front of the dog. If she starts to move, say "*Anhhh!*" If this works, praise quietly; if not, reposition without giving another command and quietly praise when Star is staying.

If verbal corrections are not sufficient, use a leash. After a few seconds, return and release, using your release word, praise and play. As you progress, gradually increase your stay time to a few minutes and then increase your distance from him until you are 30 feet away. For dogs that continue to move after repeated gentle assistance, a physical correction is warranted.

When your dog is steady on a stay for several minutes at 30 feet, begin adding distractions such as a new location, strange sights and sounds or temptations with food or toys. Use your imagination. When you start "proofing," stay close to your dog so you can prevent moving during a stay. Proofing with distractions can be very stressful, so be patient with each new situation and give extra rewards for a job well done.

THE *COME* COMMAND

No command is more important to your success in Agility than the come command. When your dog is headed for the ring gate after having run only half the course, a reliable response to the come command will save your "team" from being eliminated. The come command (sometimes called the recall) is also an essential tool for guiding or "handling" your dog between obstacles.

A dog that "sort of knows" the recall is one that is unpredictable and undependable in the ring. This could be because you neglected to proof, or perhaps you have done your proofing but have not enforced the command fairly and consistently.

To make recalls a positive experience from the beginning, start a new puppy on fast, friendly comes as soon as you get home. First, use the command whenever the pup is already coming or is sure to come to you; for example, at dinner time. Always make it extremely pleasant for your dog to come toward you. When your puppy notices you and is about to run toward you, kneel down, clap and command "*Come,*" pet and praise. Have a treat ready to make the arrival really special. After several pleasant experiences with the recall exercise, your puppy will look forward to hearing the come command.

When the dog is older, use a 6-foot lead and begin practicing more formally. In a room with no distractions, using your dog's favorite reward, your dog will probably come on your first command every time. If not, gently help the pup understand what you want, then reward. Practice no more than four to five recalls in a single session to maintain or increase the dog's enthusiasm for the exercise.

Gradually add distractions to your recalls—children or adults with food and/or toys, strange sounds and sights, etc. Practice in a wide variety of noisy public places on-lead. The first time the dog succumbs to a distraction, firmly but gently show what you wanted by pulling on the lead and praising. It is an honest mistake if you never told the dog to obey under these circumstances. If your dog continues to ignore your command, however, and behaves as if she feels she has a choice, apply a correction. A quick, sharp pop and release on the dog's collar is appropriate for most dogs. If the dog keeps ignoring your command, your correction wasn't strong or immediate enough. Let your dog know that you will give only one command, which must be responded to without hesitation. One good, strong correction can prevent you from needing to give twenty additional nagging corrections later.

After the swift, significant correction, get back on your merry way as if nothing had happened. Correcting is a very impersonal thing if done properly. It's simply cause and effect—oops . . . this is what happens when you do this—it's just the way life is!

A variation on the recall exercise is the "Come-Fore." With your dog heeling, walking or running on-lead beside you, suddenly give the command to come and begin running backward. Apply a physical correction such as a leash pop if the dog fails to comply. Praise and reward when the dog reaches you.

The dog must learn that responding to the come command is not optional—it may save your dog's life someday, so be consistent and calm in expecting compliance *every time*. "Come" is a strong, compulsive command, so don't use it indiscriminately around the house. An informal "C'mere" means "I'd like you to come here." Use "Come" around the house only when you need the dog to come immediately, and only when you are in a position to enforce the command if disobeyed.

OTHER USEFUL COMMANDS

Although you can do a respectable job in the Agility ring using only the come, sit, down and stay commands, those seeking to compete at top levels can benefit from using a few additional commands. These include "Heel," "Easy," "Go-Out," "Right" and "Left."

The Heel Command

When your dog is heeling, she should be walking or running along with you on your left side with the right ear in line with your left leg. Having a dog that is trained to heel is handy when walking to the start line and walking out of the ring, and for maneuvering around the course when you want your dog to avoid taking obstacles. Commanding a trained dog to heel not only brings the dog directly to your left leg but keeps the dog at your side until you release or give another command.

A few people who train for competitive Obedience are reluctant to use the heel command in Agility. They fear it will have a negative effect on their heeling in the Obedience ring since in Agility precise "heel position" is not required.

I feel that dog training is highly context-sensitive. Dogs can easily distinguish the Obedience ring from the Agility ring and can just as easily tailor their responses to your expectations in each competitive sport. If you are still not convinced of this, you have at least two choices:

- Use the come command and tap your leg or keep your hand extended to keep your dog with you at your left side.
- Use the heel command and demand the same precision you would in the Obedience ring.

If your dog is already trained to heel, a fun exercise to keep heeling skills sharp for Agility is "catch-up heeling." With your dog sitting in heel position, command him to stay and go to the end of your lead with your back to your dog. Command "Heel" and step off at a brisk pace. When the dog reaches your left leg, drop down and praise profusely. You can use the "treat-held-against-your-leg" technique occasionally if your dog needs extra motivation.

The Easy Command

"Easy" is a command to slow down—useful for controlling a dog's approach to and departure from each obstacle. If you use the word "Easy" instinctively in your Agility training as you use your hands to slow forward progress, the dog will catch on to the concept eventually. For dogs that ignore the "Easy" command in Agility, despite your patient and consistent use of the command, you may want to train "Easy" as a compulsive command, apart from the time and place you practice Agility.

With your dog on-lead, take off running. Suddenly command "Easy" and slow your pace down drastically—you might even take a step backward before proceeding forward at a very slow pace. The first few times you try this your dog will probably self-correct by continuing at a running pace until reaching the end of the lead. Get your dog back to your left side with verbal encouragment and by patting your leg. A treat held against your left leg is sometimes helpful to entice the dog to keep pace with you. When the dog adjusts the pace and is moving slowly at your side, praise and release from the "Easy" command using your release word. Then repeat the accelerating—braking—accelerating—braking game, expecting the dog to remain with you at a slow pace a bit longer each time before praising and releasing.

At this point you can begin adding a signal to reinforce your command. Place your left palm about one or two feet in front of the dog at eye/nose level as you command "Easy." Maintain this signal as you proceed with your slow pace. If the dog starts accelerating prematurely, contact with your hand is a self-induced correction. As your dog catches on, graduate to off-lead practice with a tab. Then advance to off-lead proofing with distractions.

The Go-Out Command

There are times in Agility, most notably in Gamblers competition, when you are required to send your dog away from you to perform one or more obstacles alone. From time to time on such occasions, every dog loses confidence or train of thought and goes halfway to the obstacle, stops, turns and looks back at the handler for guidance. If you have the go-out command at your disposal at times like these, you have a method of sending the dog back on his way. The go-out also comes in handy for sending your dog over the finish line without you. To heighten spectator excitement, judges often end their courses with a fast-paced series of hurdles. Your dog can probably run much faster than you can, and sending her through the finish line ahead of you can be a great time-saving advantage.

Obedience trainers teach the go-out as part of the "Directed Jumping" exercise in Utility, the most advanced level of Obedience competition classes. If your dog knows the go-out through previous obedience training, you already have access to this useful tool. If not, you may want to teach the go-out to help give your "team" a competitive edge in the Agility ring. Go-out should mean "go forward in a straight line until I tell you to do something different."

In the Agility ring, the "something different" will be a command for an upcoming obstacle or a directional right or left command. For simplicity's sake,

Teaching the go-out using a target.

however, to *teach* the go-out, the "something different" you ask for will be an obedience command such as sit or down.

As is the case with most Obedience work, there are as many different methods for training go-outs as there are trainers. The following "food target" technique is just one of the many approaches you could follow.

Choose a command you will use to send your dog away from you. "Go-Out," "Away" and "Scram" are possible choices. Avoid choosing the command "Go"—it sounds too much like "No," which is apt to stop a dog. Find a hallway in your house or a place in your yard where you will be able to send your dog in a straight line for a distance of 20 to 30 feet. Get a white paper plate and place it at your target destination, preferably adjacent to a wall or fence. Show the dog that you are placing a treat on the plate and refer to the food as "Go-Out" or "Away" but do not let the dog eat the treat.

Position yourself and your dog 10 feet from the target and focus attention on the plate. Give your command and a signal (flat left hand held vertically next to your dog's eyes and pointing at the target) and send the dog to the plate. Follow a few paces behind, let Star eat the treat, then give the command to sit. Reward her again when she is sitting. With successive repetitions, try to remain in your starting position without following behind your dog and give the command to sit from a distance. Gradually increase your distance from the target to 30 feet. In doing so, move your starting position farther back—do not move the target.

Later, alternate putting the food on the plate with pretending to put the food down. When you don't put the food on the plate, follow the dog out to hand-deliver the reward. Command "Sit" and then reward when the dog is sitting. Eventually, you will need to follow out only occasionally.

Gradually make the go-out target smaller and smaller by tearing off pieces from the paper plate. As the target becomes smaller, your dog will rely more on your verbal command and signal. Eventually eliminate the plate. If your dog starts to veer off course, show where the treat was. Return to the start position and try the go-out again. You can put the food in your film can to make it easier to spot and to prevent accidental rewarding without your approval. Be sure to move to different locations each time you practice to give your dog the idea of going in a straight line rather than going for a particular spot in the area where you train.

If you encounter problems with the go-out, shorten your distance and increase the size of your target. You might also try moving to a narrower training area such as a hallway to make it difficult for your dog to become distracted or to make a mistake.

The Right and Left Commands

Although not widely used in the United States today, directional control commands to make your dog turn to the right or the left can be very useful in handling your dog at a distance. For example, you have sent your dog over two hurdles without you and the dog must make a right turn to jump the next hurdle. Having a command for right turn can be very helpful when the dog is so far from you that "Come" and "Heel" have no clear directional meaning.

For those who need a more practical approach, a training method that has enjoyed some success combines recreation with learning. As you go for walks with your dog, make frequent right-angle turns, commanding "Right" or "Left." After several training sessions, you can test your dog's response by giving a right or left command as you are walking along in a straight line. It's easiest to direct a dog that is walking ahead of you rather than walking in heel position. This isn't a problem for most dogs—they are more than happy to lead the way on a pleasure outing.

Another method works well for ball-oriented dogs. As you are walking, command "right" and throw the ball to your right. Eventually the dog should start turning in the proper direction before you throw the ball. The ball then becomes a reward rather than an incentive. For dogs that are more food-oriented than ball-oriented, fill your film can with food treats and throw it. When the dog picks it up or noses it, open the can and give the reward.

After you have taught your dog to turn left and right, remember that these commands will refer to the *the dog's* left and right—not yours. When your dog is facing you, rather than beside you, you will need to translate the commands to coincide with his point of view.

SUMMARY

While not an Obedience event, Agility requires solid teamwork. Think of your dog as your dance partner—you both contribute equally to your success in Agility, but only one of you gets to "lead." Democratic or not, that duty falls to you, since you are the only one who can read the number markers!

In developing teamwork, a foundation of basic obedience training (sit, stay, down and come) is essential. The other Obedience commands described in this chapter are "gravy" and are for handlers with extra time and determination, as well as for those who are training to win among tough competition. Whether you are training to win or just to have fun, your basic obedience training will help prevent your dog from pulling embarrassing stunts during competition, such as fouling the ring, leaving the ring or running around in circles. At the same time, your basic obedience training will give you a more well-behaved and happier pet.

One of the most rewarding aspects of Agility is the teamwork developed through sequencing.

5

Sequence Training

A FTER YOUR DOG is happily performing each of the obstacles and has learned the sit, stay, down and come commands, it is time to learn "sequencing." Sequences on an Agility course range from a simple series of obstacles in a straight line to a contorted path of sharp angles and about-turns, with a few fiendishly positioned traps added to make things interesting.

Before you begin sequencing, your dog has no notion of the real excitement that lies ahead. The dog's concept of Agility is to perform each obstacle separately as an individual challenge. As a result of obstacle training, the dog has gained confidence. Pleasurable as all this is, it pales in comparison with the accomplishment you will feel when the light bulb clicks on and your dog discovers the true nature of the "Agility game." At that point the two of you will be working together, performing obstacles at a brisk pace in a pattern that is rarely twice the same. As you move about the course, your dog will remain alert as you communicate the next obstacle to perform. Finally, at the end of your run, you and your dog will congratulate each other on an impressive display of teamwork!

Learning to perform individual obstacles to this point has required a great deal of concentration by the dog—especially for precision obstacles such as the weave poles, tire jump, see-saw, dog walk and cross-over. Many handlers get discouraged after their dogs have mastered the individual obstacles and they first attempt to perform them in a sequence—some dogs act as if they've never seen the obstacles before in their lives. The dog knows how to do them as individual obstacles, but doesn't yet know how to maintain concentration from the tunnel to the tire jump to the see-saw to the weave poles.

The road from knowing the obstacles to running an entire Agility course smoothly is an enjoyable one, focusing on two things: developing your dog's ability to concentrate through long sequences and building a common language of communication.

To develop concentration, start your sequences with two or three obstacles, *beginning with hurdles, tunnels and the pause table.* As the dog attains proficiency, make your sequences longer and gradually add the other more difficult obstacles. As with most Agility training, patience will reward you.

While moving among the obstacles, you will need a common "language" of commands to enable you and your dog to work fluidly together as a team. I refer to these as "control commands." These differ from "obstacle commands" in that they indicate directions in which you want the dog to travel, rather than obstacles you want him to perform. "Come" is the only control command your dog must know to make a respectable showing in the Agility ring. For those with more time or ambition, "Heel," "Right" and "Left" and "Go-Out" are additional control commands that can help give you a competitive edge in many situations.

In competition the obstacles are quite close together—usually 15 feet apart—and crafty judges take advantage of those tight dimensions. For you and your dog to perform your best, your timing of commands in the ring is critical. This is particularly true if you are handling a large dog or a fast medium-sized dog, who can travel 15 feet very quickly.

To give your dog time to process the command, focus on the upcoming obstacle and begin to act on the command before passing an obstacle, *you must give your next command before the dog finishes the previous obstacle.* In the case of hurdles, you may have to give your command for the next obstacle as early as the moment your dog is beginning to jump. Handlers of smaller dogs have more leeway in timing since their dogs need less room to take off and have several extra strides between obstacles.

In addition to the careful timing of commands, you will need to be judicious in using your dog's name before a command. By saying "Phideaux, Tire!" you solicit his attention, which is undesirable when you want the dog to continue in a given direction. On the other hand, it may be helpful to use your dog's name when you are commanding a change in his direction, as in "Phideaux, Come!"—which works well as long as your dog's name is short enough to say quickly. By the time you say "Boulregard, Come!" your dog may have completed several obstacles without you. If you have a superfast dog, even a short name may take too long to utter as your dog is sprinting toward an incorrect obstacle.

STRAIGHT LINE SEQUENCES

The simplest type of sequence you will encounter is that in which the next obstacle is directly in front of the dog as he completes the previous obstacle.

86

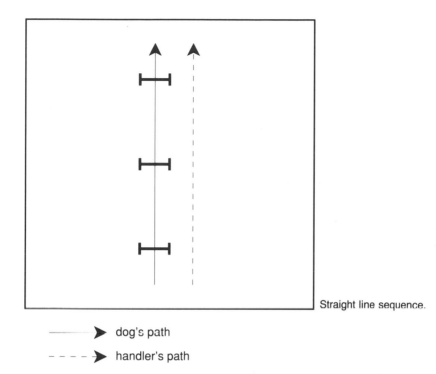

Straight line sequence.

——————▶ dog's path

- - - - ▶ handler's path

These "straight line sequences" are easily negotiated. Since there is no directional control involved, you simply give your command for the next obstacle just before the dog completes the previous one. Practicing with wide obstacle spacing at first makes it easier for both you and your dog—you have more time in which to make your command and your dog has more time to focus on the next obstacle.

At the beginning of your sequence training, before your dog has learned the rules of the Agility game, it's best to start out on a small scale. Use two single-type (rather than spread) hurdles in a straight line sequence spaced 20 to 25 feet apart and set at a lower height than your dog normally jumps. The reason for the low jump height is that you want the dog to concentrate on sequencing rather than clearing a challenging hurdle. Standing about 8 feet from the first hurdle with your dog on a 6-foot lead, get your dog's attention and perform a run-by. *When your dog is in midair,* give your command for the next hurdle, without saying his name. After several successful run-bys, take off the lead and repeat the sequence. *Don't forget to praise!*

While your dog is learning to sequence, there will undoubtedly be a few mistakes, such as trying to bypass the next hurdle. Occasionally even the best trained dogs do this in competition, so it's wise to be prepared to call the dog back and reapproach the hurdle as smoothly and quickly as possible. If Bruno balks at or begins to bypass the second hurdle, he will probably be too close to the hurdle to jump it safely on a second command without first backing up to

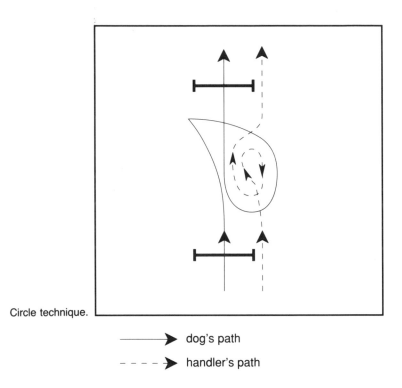

Circle technique.

——————▶ dog's path

— — — ▶ handler's path

reapproach it. If your dog is ahead of you, resist the temptation to remain stationary and facing him while calling him back to heel position. This is what most handlers instinctively do. The dog knows to jump the next hurdle and probably won't come all the way back to your left side—at least, not on your first command. If Bruno is like most dogs, you will wind up begging him and patting your leg as the seconds tick by. This puts extra stress on the dog and takes lots of time.

A smooth and efficient method of calling the dog back after a failed approach to an obstacle is one I call the "circle technique." While facing the dog, command your dog to come and position your flat left hand in front of you at your dog's eye level. (What you are trying to tell your dog is "Watch this hand.") Then turn your body in a clockwise circle, while moving your left hand to the left side of your body. This directs the dog to follow you in approximate heel position. Most often the dog will gladly go in your direction without resisting, not wanting to be left behind. With a small dog, your circle can have a very small diameter—almost a pivotal turn in place—since the dog does not need a long approach to the hurdle. The larger the dog, the larger your circle needs to be. As you complete your circle, you and your dog will be facing the next hurdle at an appropriate distance for an approach.

If your dog has completely passed the next hurdle instead of jumping it, you need to call Bruno back to reapproach the hurdle. However, take care to

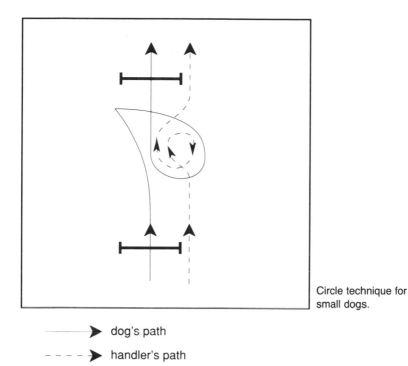

Circle technique for
small dogs.

————▶ dog's path

– – – –▶ handler's path

prevent him from taking a shortcut by jumping the obstacle on the way back. This is known as "back-jumping" and will cost you points in competition. To prevent this from occurring, keep your eye on your dog at all times and never command to come when a hurdle is between you and your dog. Instead, leap or lunge to the side of the hurdle so that you and the dog are not exchanging eye contact over the hurdle as you call.

When your dog is smoothly jumping one hurdle after the other off-lead, start moving the hurdles closer together. If your dog continues to balk at the second hurdle, increase the distance between hurdles again and then gradually move them closer together—perhaps this time in smaller increments. When your dog is jumping the hurdles smoothly at 15-foot spacings, start raising the jump heights gradually.

After your dog has mastered two hurdles at 15-foot spacing and at regulation jump height, add a third hurdle, again lowering the jump heights of all three. When the dog takes all three in succession and appears confident, gradually raise the jump heights. Then add a fourth hurdle.

At this point you can start intermixing tunnels and hurdles in your "straight line" sequences. You can also begin adding the pause table at the end of the sequences.

When using tunnels in straight line sequences, give your command for the next obstacle as soon as the dog's head emerges from the tunnel. Being inside the tunnel can be very disorienting. To help your dog regain his bearings and know immediately on which side of you to be working, have your flat hand extended so that the dog sees it at the moment of exit. Practice your sequences working off the right as well as the left.

When your dog has mastered straight line sequences using hurdles, tunnels and tables, begin including contact obstacles, weave poles and the tire jump. Remember to lower your hurdles whenever you set up complicated sequences so that your dog can concentrate on the sequence instead of the jump height. If you run into problems, back up a few steps in your training to a point where your dog is performing happily and accurately. Then slowly increase the difficulty level to preserve confidence.

STRAIGHT LINE SEQUENCES WITH CALL-OFFS

Next, it is time to make Agility more interesting (and even more fun!) by throwing your dog a curve. In competition, there will be times when the obstacle immediately in front of your dog's nose is *not* the obstacle you want the dog to take. Judges deliberately set "traps" by placing enticing but incorrect obstacles in the dog's logical path. Handling your dog in these trap situations requires the "call-off" technique.

To practice the call-off, arrange three hurdles in a straight line sequence with the heights set low. With your dog on-lead, run along as you command to jump over the first two hurdles, making sure you give your commands at the proper time.

As your dog is in midair over the second hurdle, command to come and start turning right. As the dog lands, continue moving right, making sure the leash does not tighten until after the landing. This is important because pressure on the leash in midair can throw your dog off-balance and cause a fall. A prompt response to your command to come will not allow the leash to tighten. Praise your partner lavishly! If the dog does not come back toward you after landing, the leash will tighten as you move away and the dog will self-correct. Praise and play when your dog reaches you, and then repeat the exercise. If the dog continues to ignore your command, resolve to practice the come command away from your Agility practice sessions.

Once your dog is responding to your call without tightening the lead, remove the lead and repeat the call-off exercise. Use abundant praise and rewards for proper behavior! If you encounter problems, put the dog back on-lead, or block the third hurdle by having someone stand in front of it. Reward for a successful performance even though you have made it difficult for your dog to fail. If your dog persists in ignoring your call-off, get one successful performance on-lead and then quit that exercise for the day. Before resuming your sequence training, practice the come command in a variety of distracting conditions.

Some handlers take the easy way out when they encounter problems by

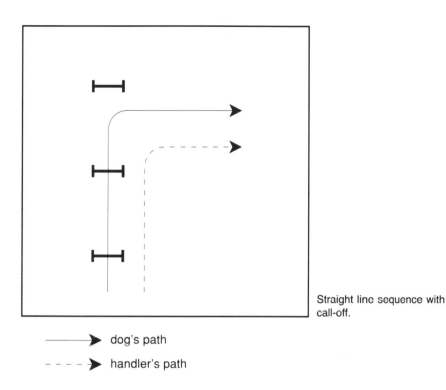

Straight line sequence with call-off.

──────▶ dog's path

- - - - ▶ handler's path

continuing most of their training on-lead. I believe in taking the dog off-lead as soon as possible after you begin sequencing for a variety of reasons:

- Dragging your dog from obstacle to obstacle isn't nearly as much fun for either of you as is developing teamwork off-lead.
- Off-lead handling is safer since you don't have the possibility of snagging your lead on an obstacle. It's almost impossible to keep up with a fast dog without inadvertently pulling back on the lead, which can throw the dog off balance, alter jumping technique or damage confidence.
- Your dog will learn to take obstacles in sequence faster if you train off-lead. With the lead on your dog doesn't have to think as much or make as many decisions. To the dog the rules of the "Agility game" become "we are going to run from obstacle to obstacle and I will feel pressure on my collar that will tell me where to go next." As a result the dog does not learn to pay attention to your commands and signals, and when the lead finally does come off, the dog is lost.

For the best results, train your dog to respond to the come command consistently *before you begin sequencing*, and then use the lead only for the purpose of showing the dog what you want done. Then do it off-lead.

When your dog is performing call-offs reliably without your lead, alternate sending the dog over the third hurdle with calling Bruno off at random intervals to keep him alert and thinking. Then gradually raise the jump heights.

RIGHT TURNS

In situations where the obstacle you want your dog to perform is not in the direction Phideaux is heading, you need to give the dog a command that will bring his vision in line with the next obstacle. Then you can give the command for taking that obstacle.

For most right turns you will be handling your dog off your left side because this is a much shorter path than handling off your right. Making a right turn is similar to performing a call-off.

Suppose you want your dog to jump a hurdle, make a sharp right turn and immediately jump a second hurdle. Because the second hurdle is not in the dog's field of vision as the first is jumped, you must give a control command while the dog is in midair over the first hurdle to get Phideaux to turn in the direction of the second. "Come" works well since you are positioned in the direction in which you want your dog to turn. The dog will come toward the sound of your voice. "Come" is also a good choice because it is a powerful, compulsive obedience command that has a very clear meaning to both you and your dog. If your dog understands "Heel" as a compulsive command to come directly to your left side, you can use it as an alternative to the come command.

"Heel" is beneficial when you want the dog not only to come to you but to continue moving along with you at your left side without taking any obstacles until otherwise commanded. Another alternative for those who have trained directional commands is to use the "Right" command. The benefit of this command is that it works independently of your location on the course; thus, you would not have to move toward the second hurdle to get the dog to turn right and focus on it. Such directional control can sometimes save you steps and reward you with much faster times on the course.

When the dog has veered right and is in line with the second hurdle, give a command to jump. If you have used the command "Come" or "Heel," don't make the dog come all the way to you before giving the command for the next hurdle.

You may ask, isn't it a bad idea to give a command and not require the dog to complete the action? On the contrary, you are asking the dog to do exactly what you ask, when you ask it—you are merely interrupting one command with another. Obedience examples of this include the Drop on Recall, Hang Sit and Down and the Go-Out.

When training interrupted commands, it is important to alternate randomly between requiring your dog to complete the first command (making Phideaux come all the way to you) and interrupting the command (commanding him to jump). This maintains your dog's interest, keeps him guessing and prevents his

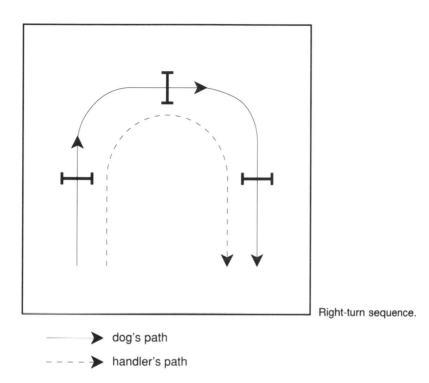

Right-turn sequence.

──────▶ dog's path

- - - - ▶ handler's path

anticipation of one situation or the other. It also prevents weakening of your control commands.

To begin teaching a right-turn sequence, it helps to break the exercise into parts. Set up three low hurdles at right angles with 20-foot spacing so that the dog's path will be a clockwise semicircle. Running alongside with your dog on your left, command and signal your dog to jump. When the dog is in midair, give your control command ("Come," "Heel," or "Right") while turning right, and stop without continuing to the second hurdle. As soon as the dog has reached your left side, bend down and praise. (It's also helpful to hold a food reward against your left leg to condition the dog to come all the way to your leg.) Then reposition yourself for the next hurdle and command your dog to jump. When the dog is in midair, give your control command, turn and again stop and reward when your dog reaches your leg.

Now you are ready to try putting it all together. Repeat the exercise except this time, instead of stopping between all of the hurdles and making the dog come all the way to you, interrupt the control command with the command for the next hurdle. If your dog bypasses or begins to bypass the hurdle, use the circle technique described for straight line sequences. If bypassing continues to be a problem, widen the distance between the hurdles so that the dog has more time to mentally prepare for the jump. If this doesn't end the bypassing, put your dog back on-lead (with hurdles still set low) and focus on making just one

Teaching the dog to watch your
signaling hand by keeping food
or a small toy in your palm.

right turn using two hurdles. Then add the third. Gradually shorten the distance until the dog is performing well with the hurdles spaced 15 feet apart. Then slowly raise the jump heights.

When Phideaux's happily performing the sequence, alternate calling him all the way to your leg with the command to jump over the second hurdle so that the dog does not become sloppy about obeying your control command.

LEFT TURNS AND HANDLING OFF THE RIGHT

Just as right turns are easiest handled off the left, left turns are most efficiently handled off the right-hand side.

For many seasoned Obedience competition dogs, handling off the right is downright uncomfortable. You may have spent the last four to six years giving your dog commands from only your left side. Now you must change the rules!

There are several ways to have your dog working from either side of you. Straight line jump sequences are a good place to start. Command a sit-stay, move behind the dog to the left, then leave your dog without crossing in front. Stand on the opposite side of the first hurdle with your back to your dog. Look at your dog over your right shoulder and extend your right arm in a flat hand signal—the signal should be visible to the dog over the hurdle. This signals that now you are working off the right. Command to jump. If the dog bypasses the hurdle, lower it. Then try again, this time positioning the dog closer to the hurdle so that it will be more inconvenient to go around it. If successful, continue with the other hurdles in the sequence. The momentum from the first jump will usually carry the dog on your right for the entire sequence.

Some dogs will perform an obstacle off your right and then will immediately return to your left side (heel position). A continuously extended right hand, held low, is helpful in keeping this type of dog on your right between obstacles. To encourage watching for your hand signal, place food or a small toy in your signaling hand and run around with your dog on your right. When he has remained on your right side for a few running steps, twist your wrist counterclockwise and give the reward. Gradually increase the amount of time you expect him to stay with you on your right before rewarding. Soon Bruno will look forward to seeing your right arm extended and become more willing to remain on your right between obstacles. (This technique also works for dogs that are reluctant to watch your left hand when working off the left.)

It is sometimes difficult to position the dog on your right to begin an off-the-right sequence, especially if you are in the middle of a course run and not starting from a standstill. This can happen when your dog does something un-expected and winds up a few feet in front of you and facing you, in a poor position to begin a sequence. Teaching a command to get your dog on your right side facing your direction can help save you time on the course. This is a great "rainy day" exercise you can practice inside the house using food or a tennis ball for motivation.

Teaching the cross command.

Choose a command such as "Cross" or "This side." With your dog out a few feet in front of you, hold a reward in your right hand in front of the dog's nose. Give your command as you move the reward to your right side. Give the reward when the dog is in the equivalent of heel position on your right side. (You can use the same exercise on your left to teach the dog to come to heel position from a position in front of you using the command "Heel.")

Making Left Turns

Break the exercise into parts. Set up three hurdles at right angles with 20-foot spacing so that the dog's path will be a counterclockwise semicircle. Running alongside your dog, command and signal to jump. When he is in midair, give your control command while turning left and stop without going on to the second hurdle. As soon as Bruno has reached your right side, stop and reward.

When calling the dog to your right side, do not use the heel command, since this will bring the dog to your left leg. If you have trained the left command, use it. If not, use the come command. Then reposition yourself for the next hurdle and command your dog to jump. When he's in midair give your control command, turn, and again stop and reward as your dog reaches your leg.

As you did when teaching right turns, try the entire sequence without

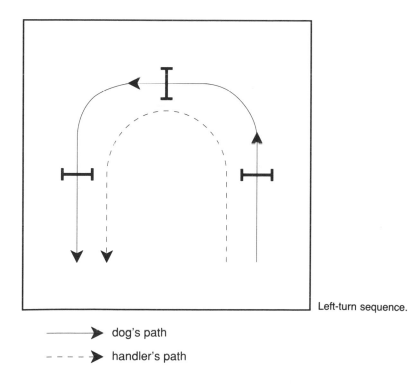

Left-turn sequence.

⎯⎯⎯⎯▶ dog's path

- - - - ▶ handler's path

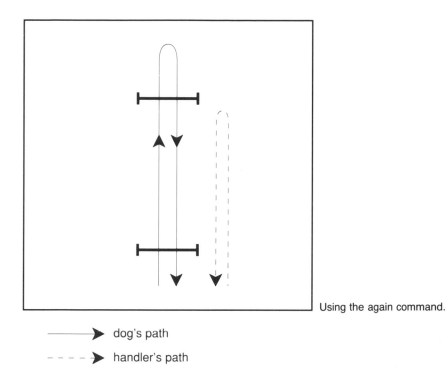

Using the again command.

———————▶ dog's path

- - - - ▶ handler's path

past the hurdle for several practice sessions until Phideaux catches on. For stubborn cases, you may need to throw a reward over the hurdle to encourage him to jump ahead of you. When the dog touches the ground, clap your hands to get attention while simultaneously commanding "Come—Again." Then quickly extend your right arm in a clear jump signal. As the dog has turned toward the hurdle, give your jump command. The reason you don't begin commanding in midair, at least at first, is that some dogs are so responsive to the come command that they neglect to go out far enough to have adequate room to approach the hurdle. After several sessions of commanding "Come—Again—Jump," begin eliminating the clapping and the jump command so that you are just commanding "Come—Again." Then gradually drop the "Come." Eventually the dog will respond to the again command by turning in his tracks and repeating the previous obstacle.

Practice the same maneuver, except this time switch to the other side of the hurdle while your dog is jumping away from you.

To keep your dog thinking and to keep training fun, alternate randomly between calling him back over the hurdle and calling him around it. Call him around by leaping or lunging to the side of the hurdle and commanding "Come." It can help to bend down and clap your hands at the dog's eye level to get attention. (Never command the dog to come while exchanging eye contact with your dog over a hurdle. If you do, he will most likely jump it on his way back

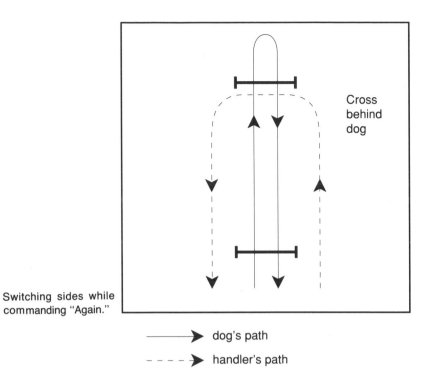

Cross
behind
dog

Switching sides while
commanding "Again."

———————▶ dog's path

- - - - ▶ handler's path

to you.) Then set up a second hurdle 15 feet away and in a straight line with the first. To teach Phideaux that he must respond to your commands rather than a set pattern of behavior, alternate between the series of two hurdles and calling back over the first, using the again command.

The real beauty of the again command, as opposed to the come command, is that it works wherever you may be on the course. When you begin working your dog from a distance, "Again" will mean "Take the previous obstacle" regardless of your position in relation to the dog. Expect your dog to be insecure about this at first; you may need to help him through it and encourage Phideaux back over the hurdle. Throwing a ball or a food-filled film can over the hurdle away from you may help give the dog an extra incentive.

SWITCHING SIDES

You can decrease the amount of time it takes you and your dog to run a course if you, the handler, take the shortest path possible. This often requires you to make midcourse switches from handling off the left to handling off the right, and vice versa.

Switching sides while the dog is performing a tunnel or contact obstacle is an easy maneuver. As soon as the dog has committed to the obstacle, quickly cross behind it and be ready to handle off the opposite side as the dog completes the obstacle.

Switching sides during jump sequences is much more difficult, however, and requires careful planning on your part before running the sequence with your dog. The techniques you use depend on whether you are switching sides during a straight line sequence or during a right or left turn.

During Straight Line Sequences

Sometimes you need to switch sides while performing a straight line sequence because of the arrangement of obstacles on the course. For example, you may have approached the straight line from your right and need to exit from your left. You can handle this smoothly without slowing down your dog or giving any control commands by switching behind or in front of your dog while between two of the obstacles in the straight line.

Whether you switch in front of or behind your dog depends on the speed of your dog, how confident Bruno is when working ahead of you and the type of obstacles in the sequence. If your dog is not extremely fast and the obstacles are the type that take extra time to complete, such as the collapsed tunnel, you

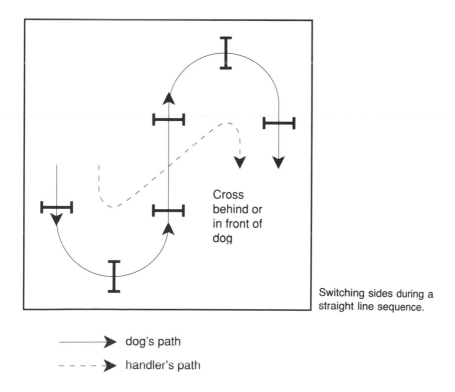

Cross behind or in front of dog

Switching sides during a straight line sequence.

———▶ dog's path

- - - -▶ handler's path

101

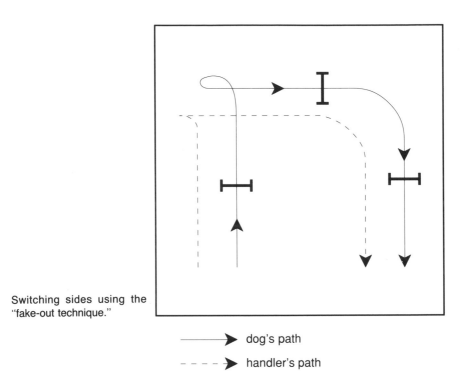

Switching sides using the
"fake-out technique."

———→ dog's path

- - - -→ handler's path

may be able to smoothly switch sides in front of him. Otherwise, it is usually best to switch behind the dog. Make sure you extend your arm in a flat hand signal immediately after you switch sides so that the moment your dog catches a glimpse of you, he knows on which side of you to work.

During Right and Left Turns

There are several methods you can use to switch from your right to your left, depending on your level of training, confidence in your dog and willingness to take risks.

One of the most conservative approaches is the one I call the "fake-out technique." To practice this technique, use the same configuration you use to teach the right turn—three low hurdles set up at right angles with 20-foot spacing. With your dog on your right, give a command and signal to take the first hurdle. When your dog is in midair, give the control command "Come" as you turn to your left with your right arm extended indicating that the dog stay on your right for the turn. Make an abrupt 180-degree pivot in place and extend your left arm. Now your dog is on your left and your left hand is informing your dog that it is now working off your left. Complete the remaining two hurdles off your left. When performed correctly, the fake-out technique takes very little time, and gives you the peace of mind that you have aligned your dog properly with the

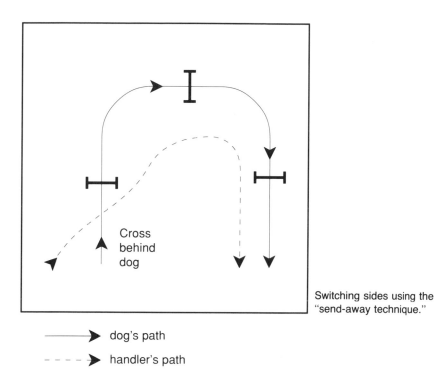

Cross
behind
dog

Switching sides using the
"send-away technique."

———————➤ dog's path

- - - - ➤ handler's path

hurdle and have given it an adequate approach. As a result, you have decreased the likelihood that your dog will bypass the hurdle or displace a bar or board while jumping.

Side Switching in Higher-Level Classes

In the higher-level classes, the fast speeds required may convince you to take greater risks to gain more competitive times. A more aggressive "send-away technique" requires that your dog be fast and comfortable performing an obstacle ahead of you. It also helps if the dog is responsive to the go-out command as well as to the right and left commands. To practice the send-away technique, use three hurdles in the same configuration as for the fake-out technique. With your dog on your right, command and signal for the first hurdle. Let Bruno go out over the hurdle while you cross behind. When he has traveled far enough to jump the second hurdle, extend your left arm and command "Come" or "Right" to get him to make the right turn; then command to jump as soon as the next hurdle is in his field of vision. Continue over the third hurdle off your left.

This send-away technique works only if your dog goes out in a straight line and far enough over the first hurdle to give an adequate approach to the second. If not, you can use your go-out command when he is in midair over the first hurdle, then interrupt with a come or right command when the dog is in line with the next hurdle.

The same options and procedures apply in reverse for starting a left turn sequence with your dog on your left.

NEGOTIATING TRAPS

A trap situation is, by definition, preventing your dog from taking an obstacle out of sequence. Most judges deliberately include a few traps in every course to provide a challenge and to test the amount of control and teamwork you have developed with your dog. Spectators love the suspense of traps, too!

The key to negotiating traps is to plan how you will handle them *before* you attempt the sequence with your dog. At a competition you will always have an opportunity to walk the course without your dog before you run it with your dog. This is the time to identify any traps and analyze them from your dog's point of view. Then plan exactly what commands you will give, when you will give them and where you will position yourself to decrease the likelihood that your dog will succumb to the traps. In your training sessions, use your imagination to set up devious trap sequences to give you and your dog the experience of dealing with them.

Most traps fall into one of two categories: an incorrect obstacle placed

A typical "trap."

directly in your dog's path, or two or more obstacles placed close to one another—only one of which is correct. The handling technique you choose depends largely upon the type of trap and the skill level of your dog.

Obstacle in Dog's Path

Imagine your dog flying over a spread-bar jump and seeing the pause table directly in his path. Unfortunately, the pause table is not the next designated obstacle in the course; instead, you are to make a sharp right turn to take the collapsed tunnel. How do you prevent your dog from taking the table?

Leave your dog at the start line and stand between the hurdle and the pause table to block your dog's view of the table. Call him over the hurdle and then start moving toward the tunnel while commanding and signaling to perform the tunnel—which is the correct obstacle. Always remember when using blocking techniques such as these that if your dog runs into you while you're obviously attempting to block him, you will incur faults for touching your dog.

Since most traps are not positioned at the start, they are usually not this easy to handle. If you are running with your dog in the above example, you must rely on a call-off. Start the jump with your dog on your left. When he is in midair, turn toward the tunnel and command "Come" or "Right." Then command Bruno to the tunnel when it is in his field of vision. If it is not reasonable to work the spread-bar jump with your dog on your left, you must rely on either the "fake-out" or the "send-away" technique for switching sides.

If your dog does not respond immediately to your call-off, say "*Anhhh, Come!*," or just "Come" if your dog is very fast and responsive to the command. The *Anhhh!* often convinces the dog to stop in its tracks, knowing something is wrong. Be sure to use a firm tone of voice when calling your dog off a trap—a soft or half-hearted command is sometimes ignored by a determined dog.

Obstacles in Close Proximity

When two obstacles are side by side and only one is correct, your handling largely depends on your side of approach. Consider this example: you are approaching a trap in which the pipe tunnel entrance is placed left of and a foot away from the dog walk. The next obstacle you are to take is the dog walk, and you can handle the trap in one of two ways: (1) Keep the dog at a controlled pace on your right as you run alongside, blocking the view of the tunnel as you approach the dog walk, or (2) send the dog ahead of you, using your command for the dog walk and relying on your dog's training to distinguish between obstacles on voice command only (discussed later in chapter 6, Distance Control).

The latter option can save you time with a fast, highly trained dog, although it entails a large amount of risk. In advanced-level classes you run the risk of an additional point deduction: If your dog becomes confused and turns back to look at you instead of taking the dog walk as commanded, the dog incurs faults

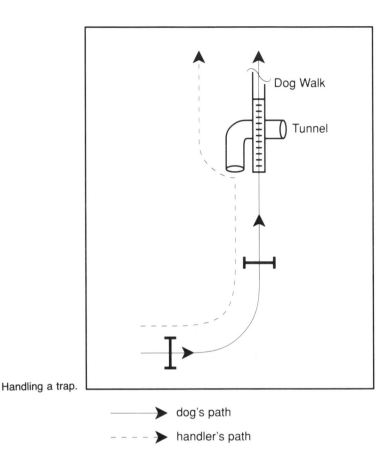

Handling a trap.

———————▶ dog's path

– – – – ▶ handler's path

for a "refusal" or may take an incorrect obstacle. On the other hand, if all goes smoothly you've probably saved yourself a good bit of time and have pulled off an impressive feat.

Consider the same hypothetical situation, but this time the pipe tunnel is the next obstacle in the sequence. You could choose option number two (send your dog ahead) if your dog can distinguish the tunnel from the dog walk by verbal command alone, or you can use a technique to "handle" the trap. Because you are approaching the trap with your dog on your right, you will not be able to block the dog's view of the dog walk without first switching sides. To do so you can use a circling maneuver to switch from handling off the right to handling off the left. When the dog is in midair over the last hurdle in the sequence, turn clockwise to face the dog as you give a command to come. As the dog approaches you, show your left hand and turn clockwise to face the tunnel after the switch. The dog will be on your left, in a good position for you to control its approach and to block its view of the dog walk.

Even with smooth, well-planned handling, your dog may become bound

106

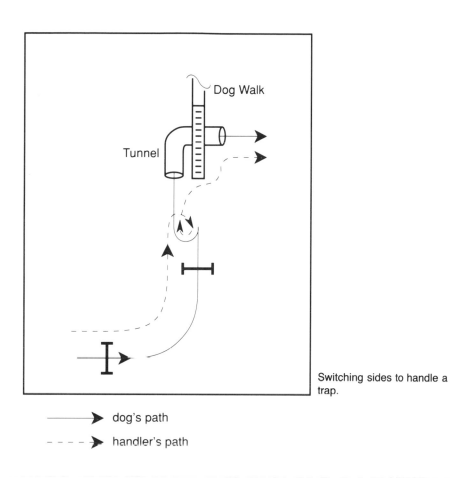

Switching sides to handle a trap.

———→ dog's path

- - - -→ handler's path

and determined to take the incorrect obstacle. The number one rule of Agility applies here—*always keep an eye on your dog.* The moment he begins eyeing an incorrect obstacle, command "*Anhhh*, Come!" and redirect the dog to the correct obstacle. Some dogs respond more promptly to the command to down from a distance than they do to the come. You can drop these dogs before they reach the incorrect obstacle and then position yourself to block the trap before you release them.

PROBLEMS WHILE SEQUENCING

Sometimes you may think your dog understands how to properly perform an obstacle, until you discover that the dog can't perform it under the stress of a sequence.

When sequencing problems occur during your training sessions, stop, analyze and correct them. These difficulties assume a wide variety of forms,

107

and there is never just one solution—you may have to try several approaches before finding one that works with your dog. *Always blame the dog last*. It's tough to admit it, but most sequencing failures are caused by handling errors or by mistakes made while training. No book can cover every training challenge; however, some common sequencing problems and possible solutions are described below.

Dog Habitually Bypasses Obstacles

First, rule out sore paw pads or lameness. After these are ruled out, consider handler-caused problems. Make sure your obstacle commands have been given early enough by having others watch you or by videotaping yourself. If your commands have been given sufficiently early, ensure you haven't been using your dog's name on straight line sequences. This can cause your dog to look at you instead of focusing ahead toward the next obstacle. On turns, check that you are giving your dog enough room to approach the next obstacle and that your approach is head-on.

In many cases, the dog is merely inexperienced. Return to basics by practicing with two hurdles at a low height, 20 feet apart with your dog on-lead. Gradually decrease the distance between hurdles and increase jump heights, and then progress to off-lead work.

Dog Repeatedly Jumps on Handler

The dog may be insecure from inexperience or may have developed a habit of ''fawning'' over the handler. In either case, *never* praise, pet or reward your dog while it is jumping on you during a sequence. In extreme cases, discourage the behavior using a correction followed by immediate praise when the dog is no longer jumping on you. Try keeping a toy or food-filled film can in your outstretched signaling hand to encourage the dog to focus on your signal. When doing this, occasionally throw the object straight ahead to reward good performances (rather than rewarding the dog when he comes to you).

Dog Habitually Leaves the Ring

If your dog leaves the ring while you are working, regardless of the reason, he is ignoring a control command to come, since you undoubtedly call him the moment he heads for the ring gate. To eliminate this problem, work on your recalls both on- and off-lead, apart from your Agility training. In your practice sessions set Phideaux up in increasingly distracting situations until his response is automatic.

Sometimes a dog that leaves the ring is displaying avoidance, possibly because of a stressed condition. *Analyze your methods to ensure that you have been patient and fair*. If you have, your dog may just be reacting strongly to the stress that is a natural part of learning. Have patience with the inexperienced dog by calmly insisting on the completed action you requested before he fled. If this avoidance behavior continues over many practice sessions, despite the dog being very familiar with the actions you request, it is time to apply a correction. Leaving the ring during competition is an automatic elimination and, therefore, a behavior you want to stop.

Sometimes a dog leaves the ring to flee to the lap of another person, frequently a spouse. When this happens, it is critical that the recipient of the dog's attentions does not encourage or reward the dog in any way. All too often, the spouse thinks it's "cute" for Phideaux to come running for protection and inadvertently encourages the dog to repeat the offense later, when the going gets tough again.

Dog Stops to Urinate

Nip this one in the bud as soon as possible! Urinating in the ring is another offense that is cause for instant elimination from competition. Besides, it makes an unflattering statement about the level of teamwork you and your dog have achieved.

Make sure you have offered Phideaux a chance to relieve himself before beginning to work. If you are innocent and have ruled out a medical problem such as a bladder infection (which is not likely, but possible), it's safe to blame and correct the dog. An immediate stare-down and shaking is appropriate. Although many dogs urinate to mark their territories as a "macho" ritual they feel compelled to perform, it is an affront to you as team leader and is totally unacceptable behavior while you are working together as a team.

Dog Stops to Sniff

It's natural for dogs to want to sniff, so don't discourage it completely; however, never allow sniffing while under a command. When you have given your dog a command and Phideaux starts to sniff, lift up on and hold the muzzle while commanding "*Anhhh!*—No-Sniff!" For your dog to understand the connection between the sniffing and your reprimand, you must be immediate and extremely consistent in correcting the behavior *every time* it occurs during a command.

To prepare for any situation, it pays to teach your dog never to eat food off the floor. This involves deliberately littering the floor of a practice area with food and correcting the dog whenever he grabs for it. If Phideaux resists the food, pick it up and give it to him. Eventually, when your dog sees food on the ground, he will look at you rather than the food, since he will have learned that you are the source of his reward.

Dog Barks Continuously

Some dogs are prone to barking during the excitement of Agility. Although your dog won't receive a point deduction for excessive barking in the ring, a yapping dog can have trouble hearing your commands. Barking can also be a sign of dominance, indicating that your dog doesn't really believe that you are in charge.

To remedy the problem, teach the dog a command such as "That's enough!" or "Hush!" away from Agility, when the dog is barking at home. After allowing him a few barks, tell him "That's enough," and clamp the muzzle closed for a few seconds; then praise and release. If Phideaux continues yapping, repeat the process, holding the muzzle for a longer period.

All sorts of creative solutions can be tried for stubborn cases—a sharp shake of a metal can filled with coins, or a squirt in the mouth with reconstituted lemon juice from one of those plastic lemons—anything that will make him temporarily stop barking. Then praise and reward the dog for being quiet. Gradually increase the length of time you expect him to be quiet on one "That's enough" command.

When the command is working well at home, try using it during Agility training the moment the dog starts to bark while working. If he doesn't comply, stop what you are doing and correct immediately. If he does comply, stop what you are doing and reward immediately. The next time Phideaux starts barking, give your command. If he complies, praise him and continue with one obstacle, then stop and reward him. Gradually increase the length of time you expect him to be quiet for the reward, and later only reward him randomly. If at any time the dog reverts and does not respond to your command, stop and correct immediately.

As an alternate method, a two to five minute down-stay may take the wind out of a yappy dog's sails. If he learns that barking means an end to his fun, Phideaux might think twice about barking.

Dog Slides Off Pause Table

Although your dog may never have slid off the table when practicing the individual obstacles, once the dog is in the throes of a fast-moving sequence, this can happen.

The conservative approach is to "handle" your dog up to the table. When you know you will be approaching the table from a fast-paced jump sequence or after charging out of a tunnel, you should be prepared to slow your dog down considerably—perhaps even heel your dog up to the table before giving your command. This approach will slow down your time on the course, but it greatly decreases the likelihood that you will lose points for sliding off the table.

A more aggressive approach is to set up a situation in which the dog slides off the table during practice so you can discourage this. Begin by setting up a very fast-paced sequence that runs directly into the table. If you have an intelligent and cooperative dog, say "*Anhhh!*" as it slides off the table and then call the dog back on. For other dogs, place a mound of chicken wire or another unpleasant (but not dangerous) surface behind the table. When your dog slides off it will land on that surface and probably won't want to repeat the mistake.

As an alternative, you could place a sheet of clear plastic perpendicular to the back edge of the table—an invisible wall that the dog hits if it travels too far. Despite all your preparation, none of this will do any good unless you can get the dog to slide off in practice. If the fast-paced sequence doesn't do the trick, have someone throw a tennis ball or toy while you are sending the dog to the table to lure it into sliding off the opposite side.

SUMMARY

The true essence of the "sport" of Agility is not the performance of individual obstacles. Rather, it's the smooth teamwork of dog and handler as they move together, yet independently, on the Agility course. To get the most out of your dog while you are sequence training, keep the following thoughts in mind:

- Present your dog with only one "challenge" at a time. When training a new sequencing maneuver, begin using single-type hurdles, set at a low height with wide obstacle spacing. Then begin narrowing the spacing and then raising the jump heights. Finally, you can add more difficult obstacles to your sequences.
- For your dog's safety and to encourage independent thinking, try to work off-lead as soon as possible. If the dog is out of control when off-lead, suspend your sequence training until your dog reliably comes to you on your first command.
- Remember to practice your sequences with your dog on your right as well as on your left. This flexibility is a tremendous advantage in the Agility ring.
- Problems arise in any kind of training, so expect a few setbacks along the way in your Agility work. Give your dog the benefit of the doubt when you are unsure whether it understands your commands. Help the dog through periods of confusion or fear by gently showing what you had in mind. By the same token, don't be afraid to correct deliberate disobedience decisively. Your dog may need to be reminded occasionally that you are the leader of your team.

Controlling your dog at a distance allows you to take shortcuts and make faster times on the course.

6

Distance Control

HAVEN'T YOU DREAMED of being able to stand in the middle of the ring, directing the dog through a series of obstacles while remaining perfectly cool, calm and collected? With a bit of practice you should be able to send your dog ahead of you through simple sequences, at the very least, allowing you to take shortcuts, save steps and make faster times. Dogs can usually run faster than their owners—they consider humans a handicap!

Sending your dog ahead of you has another practical advantage—it prepares you to perform the "gamble" in the Gamblers class. If you choose to attempt the gamble, you will be sending your dog away from you through a series of obstacles in a very limited amount of time. Not only must your dog be willing to work away from you, it must remain steady and work quickly amidst the cheering of hordes of excited spectators.

By now you should be able to send your dog on a single command and signal from either your right or left side to the pause table, pause box, pipe tunnel and collapsed tunnel from a distance of 20 to 30 feet. If you have been especially ambitious in your training, you should also be able to send your dog through the weave poles without you. This now becomes your foundation for advanced work on control at a distance.

PERFORMING "GAMBLES"

Some of the most challenging fun you can experience in Agility is teaching your dog to complete a series of obstacles away from you, as required when you choose to perform a "gamble." There are no restrictions on the type or number of obstacles that can be included in a gamble sequence—it is limited only by the judge's imagination and good judgment. Most gamble sequences, however, involve two to four obstacles and often end with a pause table.

To begin training gambles, refresh your dog's memory by sending her to the table from a distance of 30 feet. When Star is doing this reliably, place a hurdle about 10 feet from the table with the height set low. With your dog off-lead and at your side, approach the hurdle at a run and command to jump while you remain behind the hurdle. When the dog is in midair and facing the table, give your command for the table. Don't make the mistake of waiting until your dog has landed. If your command is late, the table will no longer be in her field of vision and she will look at you quizzically when you give a command for the table. Be careful not to use the dog's name before your table command, as this may also cause her to turn back and look at you.

If your dog stops after jumping the hurdle, turns toward you and looks confused, you can use your *Go-Out* command and signal (if you have taught them to your dog) to send her back toward the table, followed by the *Table* command. If you have not taught the go-out, run to the table and show what you wanted by tapping the table enthusiastically. After Star is on the table, praise and then release. Allow her to watch you place a treat on the table. Take her back to the other side of the hurdle and repeat the process. Have an assistant stand near the table to be ready to snatch up the reward if your dog decides to go around rather than over the hurdle. Block the sides of it so she cannot go around on the next try.

When Star starts catching on, walk out to the table as usual but this time only pretend to place a reward on the table. Send your dog over the hurdle to the table, this time rewarding from your hand when the dog is on the table. From this point onward, reward this way unless she regresses. Eventually eliminate the step of pretending to put the food on the table and reward only randomly. Work toward moving the hurdle to 15 feet in front of the table, and then work on raising the jump height. Expect possible setbacks when raising the jump height, since it takes a lot more confidence for your dog to jump away from you where she cannot see what is on the other side.

After she has mastered the exercise using one type of hurdle, switch to another. It's best to start with single-type jumps and graduate to spread-type jumps such as the long jump, double-bar jump and spread-bar jump. Then send your dog through the tire to the table. Don't ask Star to perform the tire at a lowered height, however, since timing and technique have been calibrated for full height—the dog could misjudge the height and crash into the side of the tire.

Next, try sending the dog ahead of you through the pipe tunnel to the table. Shorten the tunnel if you encounter problems. After the pipe tunnel, try the collapsed tunnel. Beware of talking to your dog or cheering while she is inside the chute pushing away from you. The dog may hear your voice from behind and get tangled in the chute. If Star has trouble traveling straight through the chute without you, you may have to place a reward about 4 feet past the exit before sending her through.

Hurdles, tires, tunnels and the pause table are the obstacles most often used in gambles, but the pause box and weave poles are used occasionally. Although they are not common today, it would not be surprising to see the contact obstacles included in gambles in the near future, so it's best to train for all possibilities! (The big challenge with contact obstacles in gambles is ensuring that the dog touches the contact zones on both sides of the obstacle when at a distance from the handler. Using contact zone hoops consistently can help get the point across.) In your two-obstacle gamble sequences, start substituting the pause box for the pause table; then substitute the weave poles and contact obstacles for the hurdle, tire or tunnel.

When your dog has mastered two-obstacle gambles, you can advance to three-obstacle gambles. Begin by using a straight line sequence consisting of hurdles set at a low height and a pause table, spaced 15 feet apart. Then progress

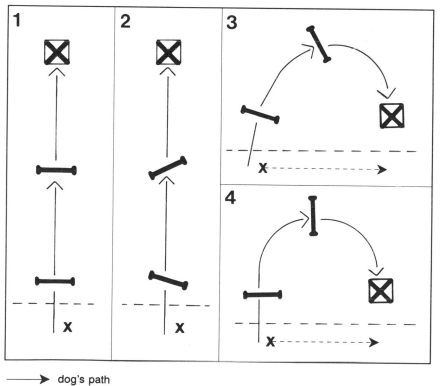

⟶ dog's path

X- - - ➤ handler's path

Progressively angling the obstacles in the gamble.

gradually to more difficult obstacles and higher jump heights as you did when training two-obstacle sequences.

Be sure to position the obstacles directly in line with one another at first so that the dog immediately sees a head-on approach to the next obstacle. When your dog gains confidence, you can begin angling the obstacles slightly so the dog has to work harder to approach each obstacle. Eventually, you can increase the angles so that the dog must change direction during the gamble sequence. Repeat the training process using four obstacles. When your dog becomes proficient, return to practicing two-obstacle gambles and add distractions.

During a competition, the gamble often brings crowds to a frenzy, so your dog needs to be prepared to ignore the sounds of the crowd and concentrate on your commands. Ask your fellow students or teammates to cheer loudly, mill around the ring, throw tennis balls, eat ice cream cones, yell "Where's the squirrel?", etc. (though not all at once—at least, not at first!), while you are

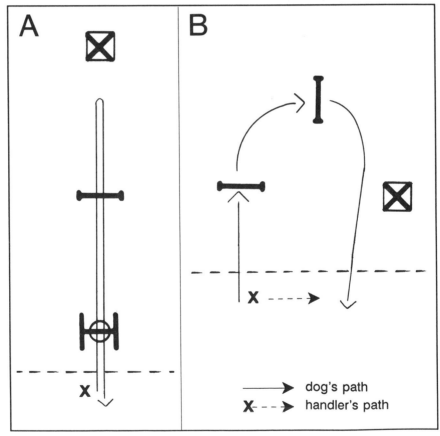

Gamble call-offs.

working on your gambles. Gradually increase the difficulty of your gamble sequences. If possible, take some of your equipment to new training locations to practice gambles in different surroundings.

To keep the game interesting and to ensure that your dog is responding to your commands rather than a set pattern, practice gamble call-offs occasionally. For example, if you have been sending your dog repeatedly through a tire, over a hurdle and to the table, now add a new variation: After the dog has jumped the tire and the hurdle, command "Again" or "Come" followed by your jump command if you have not trained the "Again" command. Get the dog to turn on the run and jump the hurdle in the opposite direction. Then call your dog back through the tire to you using your command for the tire jump. This sudden change in direction will come as a huge surprise to her the first time you try it, but Star will soon learn that the rules of the game are to listen and respond to commands. For another type of call-off, give a command to come directly to you without allowing your dog to take any obstacles in the path.

CONTROL WHILE RUNNING A COURSE

There are many times when running standard and non-standard courses other than Gamblers when control at a distance can help save you steps as well as time. These situations include sending your dog ahead of you to perform an obstacle as you take a step-saving shortcut on the course, calling her through a series of obstacles as you might at the start line or after a pause obstacle and sending Star away from you to take advantage of speed, as you would to send her over the finish line.

Distinguishing Obstacle Commands

If your dog can distinguish between obstacles on voice commands alone, you can send her ahead of you, confident that Star knows which obstacle you want her to take. To reach this level of competence, you need to start proofing your dog's recognition of obstacle commands.

Begin with the pause table and the pipe tunnel entrance side by side about 12 inches apart. Stand about 8 feet in front of the obstacles with your dog at your side, off-lead. Without signaling or moving forward, give your command for the table. What you do next depends on Star's reaction:

- If she goes to the table—praise enthusiastically!
- If she moves toward the tunnel, say "*Anhhh*! Come!" If she doesn't respond, grab her tab. (With superfast dogs, you may need an assistant to quickly step in front of the tunnel to block entering—or use a clear sheet of acrylic plastic to block the entrance.)
- If she doesn't move toward either obstacle immediately, let your com-

mand register for moment. If she still doesn't move, encourage by moving toward the table and tapping it with your hand (without giving a second command). When she is on the table, praise, then repeat.

Once the dog is patterned to go to the table, start sending her to the tunnel instead. Be prepared for a mistake. If no mistakes occur, you know that either it was an accident (unlikely, but possible) or she understands the names of the two obstacles and knows to listen to you for commands. The first time this happens is an incredibly proud moment!

Gradually increase the distance to the obstacles as well as the difficulty of the obstacles. Obviously, you can only try this exercise with obstacles that have different names—that is why you began your obstacle training by using different commands for each obstacle that appears unique to the dog.

Recognizing Signals

If you train your dog to watch for and recognize your signals from a distance, you can position yourself in strategic places on the course to call your dog through a series of obstacles.

This type of distance control is useful when leaving your dog at the start line, when you can position yourself near the third or fourth obstacle into the course to gain a head start on your dog. You can get a similar head start during

Leaving your dog at the start line and calling it through several obstacles can give you the advantage of a head start.

your dog's five-second stay on the pause table or in the pause box by moving yourself to a position several obstacles ahead as the judge counts down. Signal recognition also comes in handy during noisy situations when it is difficult to hear a verbal command.

To practice signal recognition, start by setting up two identical hurdles at a low height, side by side and 5 feet apart. Position your dog in a sit-stay about 10 feet from the hurdles and in line with the space between them. Position yourself about 15 feet away in a direct line with your dog, exchanging eye contact between the hurdles. Command and signal your dog to jump the hurdle on your right by slowly raising your right arm in a flat hand signal while leaning your body toward the hurdle on your right. If Star jumps the correct hurdle, pour on the praise! If not, what you do next depends on your dog's response:

- If she hesitates to move and is confused, help by moving toward your right with your arm still extended and establish eye contact across the correct hurdle. Encourage her by tapping the hurdle with your signaling hand, if necessary, but do not repeat your command to jump.
- If she insecurely starts to head in the right direction, praise and encourage your dog to continue.
- If she heads toward the wrong hurdle, give your *Anhhh!* correction and take her back to the starting position. Stand closer to the correct hurdle this time and try again.

When your dog is responding correctly and promptly, alternate between right and left sides until Star is confidently taking the correct hurdle on your command and signal, without your having to lean or move toward either side. Since your verbal commands for both hurdles are identical, your dog is learning to respond to your hand signal alone to determine the correct hurdle.

Next, begin eliminating the verbal command, giving only a clear, deliberate hand signal to jump. If your dog doesn't respond immediately, give the signal a moment to register. If it is still confused, tap the hurdle with your signaling hand, giving verbal encouragement. As a last resort, give a verbal command to jump. Then repeat over the same hurdle using the signal, helping only as needed. Eventually, the dog should be able to take the correct hurdle on your signal only. Gradually increase the distance and the jump heights until you have reached 40 to 50 feet with the hurdles set at full height.

Then return to your starting distances and substitute the pipe tunnel and the pause table for the two hurdles. Repeat the process, first *using both the command and the signal*. If the dog is confused, say nothing but move toward the correct obstacle with your signaling hand extended. Stop when you are touching the front of the obstacle. If you stand there silently for a few seconds, your dog will realize it was supposed to do something, and may even feel a little foolish. Praise your dog for any attempt to move toward the correct obstacle. With patience, your dog will soon catch on. Eventually, you should be able to

Proofing signal recognition.   *Photo: Gordon Simmons-Moake*

increase your distance from the correct obstacle until you are standing neutrally in between the obstacles, without leaning toward either one.

When your dog begins responding to a simultaneous command and signal from the center without your leaning toward one obstacle or the other, try *using only the signal*. You may have to decrease your distance from the obstacles at first. A common response is for the dog to stand still as if this were a test of a stay. Verbal encouragement may be needed to let your dog know it is OK to act on only a signal.

When your dog has mastered this signal-only exercise using the tunnel and table, begin substituting the tire jump, collapsed tunnel, pause box and other hurdles. If you want to get fancy, progress to the weave poles, see-saw and A-frame. When beginning with a new obstacle, give your signal and command simultaneously as you did before, and then gradually eliminate the command.

Using Go-Out and Directional Commands

Combining the go-out and directional commands (right and left), you can send your dog in a variety of directions on the course, independent of your position in relation to your dog. With this type of distance control, for example, you can send your dog across the finish line without you. You can also send your dog away from you, command a right turn and command another obstacle while you take a shortcut across the course. These slick, impressive maneuvers can save you many steps and benefit you with faster times on the course.

Along with the rewards, however, comes a substantial amount of risk. When you work with your dog via "remote control," things are great until something goes wrong. If your dog is insecure or confused and bypasses an obstacle, it can take you several seconds to run to her and get her back on track. In that time Star can easily take an obstacle out of sequence or in the wrong direction—not to mention the probability of incurring time faults for the time you spend correcting the error. In the higher-level classes you are also at a greater risk for "refusal" fault deductions when your dog is working away from you.

Plan your path so that you meet up with your dog to control her as she approaches the contact zones, and send Star only through sequences that do not contain contact obstacles. Despite the risks involved, the time savings and spectacular showmanship value make it worthwhile to work toward attaining this type of distance control on a regular basis. Once you have made progress in your training sessions, try out your new long-distance skills at matches. When your dog's performance is solid at matches, have trust in your dog and pull out all the stops during an actual competition run.

Sending Your Dog Over the Finish Line

Judges often include a fast-paced jump sequence at the end of the course to provide spectator appeal. The final fast-paced jump sequence requires the already exhausted handler to shift into an even higher gear. An alternative is to teach your dog to complete the jump sequence and cross the finish line without you.

To teach this maneuver, you need to have already trained the go-out command as described in chapter 4, Obedience Work, or by another method of your own choosing. As a result of your go-out training, you should be able to send your dog ahead of you in a straight line using one command and signal. The dog should continue in a straight line until you give another command.

Training your dog to cross the finish line does not require the use of finish markers since they will be different from trial to trial. They also may be spaced so far apart that they will not be in your dog's field of vision. Thus, it is fruitless to train your dog to recognize and head toward the finish markers. Instead, you must rely on your dog's response to the go-out command to send the dog across the finish line.

Start with one single-type hurdle set at a low height. Position a small target, such as a 1-inch piece of a paper plate with a treat on it or a film can filled with food, about 40 feet past and in a direct line with the hurdle. Don't let your dog see you position the target.

Taking a running approach to the hurdle, command and signal your dog to jump. You remain on your side of the hurdle. When the dog is in midair, give your go-out command without saying her name first. As the dog approaches the target, command a sit or down. Follow out with exuberant praise and then show where the target was and give a reward.

If the dog is confused and stops before you have given a command (which is to be expected if this is the first time you have combined jumping with a go-out command), take your dog out and show the target without any reward. Then return to the other side of the hurdle and repeat the exercise.

Gradually increase the height of the hurdle until you reach full regulation height. Then lower the hurdle and add a second low one, spaced 15 feet from the first. Repeat the exercise by commanding your dog over each of the hurdles without passing the first one, giving your go-out command when the dog is in midair over the second hurdle. Then gradually raise the jump heights. Next, lower them again and add a third hurdle, gradually working up to full height. At this point, begin angling the hurdles slightly so that the dog is still moving in an approximate straight line but has to give more thought to approaching the hurdles. By now you are undoubtedly familiar with the progression: Substitute different types of hurdles and then introduce tires and tunnels.

Taking Midcourse Shortcuts

Using distance control techniques to take midcourse shortcuts is more difficult than sending the dog through a straight line sequence since changes in direction are usually involved. You already got a taste for this in chapter 5, Sequence Training, in the discussion of the send-away technique for switching sides during a turn. Maneuvers such as these often require you to interrupt your go-out command with a directional command to turn right or left.

Up until now, most of the interrupted commands you have given your dog have been directional commands interrupted by obstacle commands—for example, "Come, Tire!" These present few problems for the dog. However, interrupting directional commands with *other* directional commands—for example, "Go-Out, Right!"—can be very confusing to the dog. Except for some Herding breeds that can capitalize on their aptitude to respond to their handlers at great distance, the use of successive directional commands is one of the most difficult maneuvers to perfect in Agility.

The diagram on page 123 shows an obstacle arrangement in which a handler's shortcut would save time when handling a fast, well-trained dog. An ideal performance would be for your dog to jump the second hurdle while you move directly to the see-saw to control the contact zones. Since the second hurdle is 25 feet away, it is unlikely that your dog would will continue far enough past the first hurdle on its own to approach the second hurdle.

Therefore, in competition you must give the go-out command while the dog is in midair. Then when your dog is in line with the second hurdle, you give a right command and follow with a command to jump when the dog is

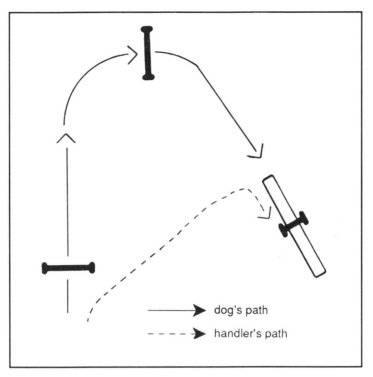

dog's path

handler's path

Taking a midcourse shortcut.

facing the second hurdle. You can then give a come command to call your dog directly to you at the see-saw.

In your training, practice each of the segments separately:

- Practice the send-away over the hurdle immediately followed by the go-out. Use a target to remind the dog to go in a long, straight line, regardless of any nearby obstacles.
- Practice just the command to turn right, followed by a command to jump. Start with the hurdles set low.
- Next, put the right turn, the second hurdle and the see-saw together.

When your dog is flawless on all of the separate parts, try it once all put together. If successful, rave like a maniac with praise!

After calling your dog off a go-out with a command to change direction, it is important to deprogram with an uninterrupted go-out. Be sure to practice the uninterrupted go-out regularly, or else your dog will begin to anticipate a change in direction and the value of the go-out will be lost. To help keep this command "pure," when you practice, do not interrupt the go out with a command to change direction more than 25 percent of the time, and preferably less frequently than that.

If your dog has a problem when you *do* put the directional commands together, gently help your dog through what you asked and then practice only the separate parts until you feel the dog is ready to give it another try. When your dog is successful, try this exercise (or a similar one of your creation) using left turn sequences handled off the right. Eventually, you can substitute spread-type jumps, tunnels and tires.

SUMMARY

Working on distance control with your dog is for those who have the ambition to excel in the Agility ring. The most advanced aspect of Agility training, achieving distance control takes patience, practice and perseverance. As a result of your training, you will be able to "ace" the most challenging gambles, call your dog through a series of obstacles and send it ahead of you with confidence as you take shortcuts on the course. Your hard work will reward you with dazzling displays of teamwork and showmanship, while forming an even better relationship of trust between you and your canine partner.

7

Training Class Ideas

SOONER OR LATER most groups that get started in Agility decide to hold training classes. Classes can help earn revenue to pay for equipment and other costs, and can introduce newcomers to the sport. Everyone benefits when new people get involved in Agility. The more people get involved, the more Agility events will be held in your area, and the more opportunities you will have to enjoy putting your training to use.

Although group training does not provide the optimum pace for every dog, it has many advantages that make it the preferred way to go. The best reason is the cost—most people can't afford private lessons. It's also more fun to learn with others with whom we can share our triumphs and setbacks. Accepting the fact that group training cannot satisfy the needs of all of the people all of the time, it is reasonable to design your training to meet the needs of the majority of students and provide extra help before and after class to those who need it.

At *FlashPaws*, we often receive calls from groups who are looking for help in planning their first training classes, as well as from those who want new ideas for existing classes. This chapter provides suggestions for structuring classes at the beginning, intermediate and advanced levels. They are only offered as suggestions—a starting point from which to base your own instruction. You will want to tailor your classes to your own preferences, available equipment, facilities and conditions.

Theoretically, developing training courses involves a simple formula: Desired skills and knowledge minus current skills and knowledge determine the content, course length and training methods.

The reality of life is that people learn Agility only if they enroll in your training program. Whenever people have a choice about whether to attend training for personal enrichment (like Agility training!), your classes need to meet their "wants" as well as their "needs." To some the payoff might be to see their dogs make rapid progress in their Agility training. Others put the highest priority on their dogs enjoying the training. Understandably, many students insist that they themselves have a good time as well! Without these payoffs, there is little chance students will continue their training.

To address students' wants and needs, our Agility classes must sometimes take departures from the most "scientific," gradual approach. While the methods described in the chapters on Obstacle Training, Sequence Training and Distance Control largely follow a practical, yet systematic approach to individual learning, the training class outlines in this chapter include compromises in the interest of allowing students to achieve as much as possible in a short amount of time.

Because of the shortcuts involved, a small percentage of students may need to repeat a level of training rather than advance with the rest of their classmates. We have found that this approach encourages people to continue their training because the dogs and handlers never get bored with a too-conservative pace.

BEGINNING AGILITY

It's important to provide ample personal attention to students at the beginning level, so it's best to keep your student/instructor ratio small. We limit our first-level classes to ten students with two instructors.

A beginner course might be structured so that, after four weeks of training, the dogs should be able to perform each of the obstacles on-lead. We require no prior obedience training to enroll in the beginner course. All obstacle training, therefore, must be on-lead. We do emphasize, however, that those who are planning to continue their training beyond the beginner level must have their dogs trained to sit, stay, down and come on command.

The classes are held for one hour per week for four weeks. Some students could benefit from a fifth week of obstacle training, but we have found that a duration of four weeks is a common psychological limit as to the time and financial commitment people are willing to make. These people are often skeptical that their dogs will be able to learn the obstacles. Once in class, however, they are amazed by how quickly and enthusiastically their dogs master them.

In our beginner classes a substantial percentage of students enroll for purposes *other than competition*—for example, as a confidence builder for their dogs or for an enjoyable night out of the house with their canine "families." To ensure an atmosphere of fun and enthusiasm, students are asked not to use verbal or physical corrections—except for cases in which the dog shows aggression toward a person or another dog.

Using two instructors, consider a "station" approach. With this approach,

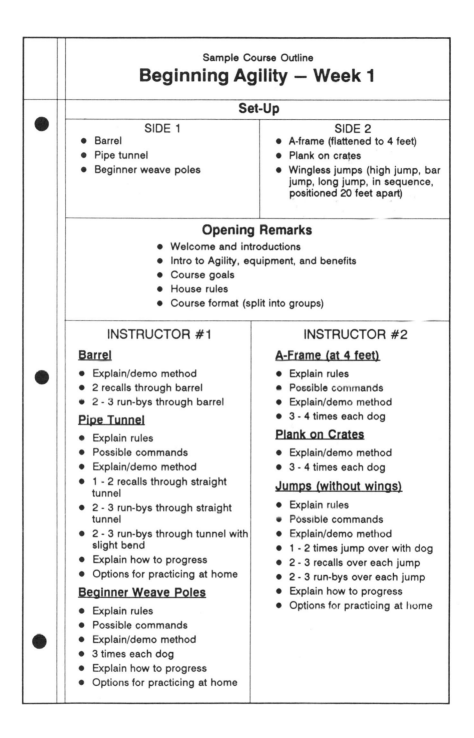

Sample Course Outline
Beginning Agility — Week 1

Set-Up

SIDE 1	SIDE 2
• Barrel	• A-frame (flattened to 4 feet)
• Pipe tunnel	• Plank on crates
• Beginner weave poles	• Wingless jumps (high jump, bar jump, long jump, in sequence, positioned 20 feet apart)

Opening Remarks

- Welcome and introductions
- Intro to Agility, equipment, and benefits
- Course goals
- House rules
- Course format (split into groups)

INSTRUCTOR #1

Barrel

- Explain/demo method
- 2 recalls through barrel
- 2 - 3 run-bys through barrel

Pipe Tunnel

- Explain rules
- Possible commands
- Explain/demo method
- 1 - 2 recalls through straight tunnel
- 2 - 3 run-bys through straight tunnel
- 2 - 3 run-bys through tunnel with slight bend
- Explain how to progress
- Options for practicing at home

Beginner Weave Poles

- Explain rules
- Possible commands
- Explain/demo method
- 3 times each dog
- Explain how to progress
- Options for practicing at home

INSTRUCTOR #2

A-Frame (at 4 feet)

- Explain rules
- Possible commands
- Explain/demo method
- 3 - 4 times each dog

Plank on Crates

- Explain/demo method
- 3 - 4 times each dog

Jumps (without wings)

- Explain rules
- Possible commands
- Explain/demo method
- 1 - 2 times jump over with dog
- 2 - 3 recalls over each jump
- 2 - 3 run-bys over each jump
- Explain how to progress
- Options for practicing at home

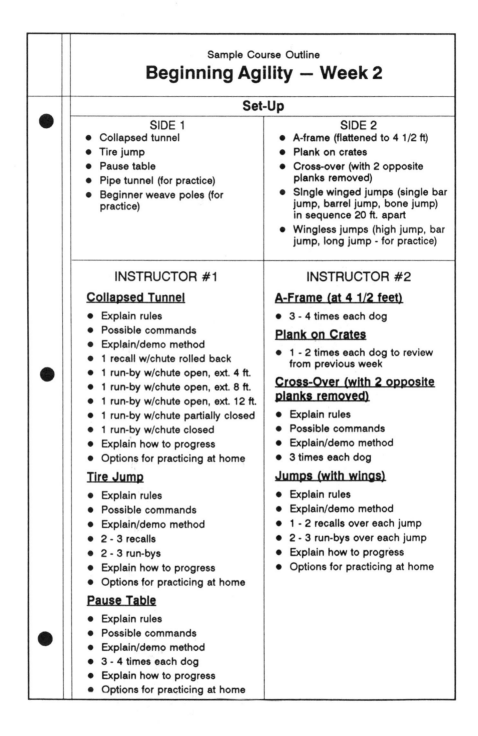

Sample Course Outline

Beginning Agility — Week 2

Set-Up

SIDE 1	SIDE 2
• Collapsed tunnel • Tire jump • Pause table • Pipe tunnel (for practice) • Beginner weave poles (for practice)	• A-frame (flattened to 4 1/2 ft) • Plank on crates • Cross-over (with 2 opposite planks removed) • Single winged jumps (single bar jump, barrel jump, bone jump) in sequence 20 ft. apart • Wingless jumps (high jump, bar jump, long jump - for practice)

INSTRUCTOR #1

Collapsed Tunnel

- Explain rules
- Possible commands
- Explain/demo method
- 1 recall w/chute rolled back
- 1 run-by w/chute open, ext. 4 ft.
- 1 run-by w/chute open, ext. 8 ft.
- 1 run-by w/chute open, ext. 12 ft.
- 1 run-by w/chute partially closed
- 1 run-by w/chute closed
- Explain how to progress
- Options for practicing at home

Tire Jump

- Explain rules
- Possible commands
- Explain/demo method
- 2 - 3 recalls
- 2 - 3 run-bys
- Explain how to progress
- Options for practicing at home

Pause Table

- Explain rules
- Possible commands
- Explain/demo method
- 3 - 4 times each dog
- Explain how to progress
- Options for practicing at home

INSTRUCTOR #2

A-Frame (at 4 1/2 feet)

- 3 - 4 times each dog

Plank on Crates

- 1 - 2 times each dog to review from previous week

Cross-Over (with 2 opposite planks removed)

- Explain rules
- Possible commands
- Explain/demo method
- 3 times each dog

Jumps (with wings)

- Explain rules
- Explain/demo method
- 1 - 2 recalls over each jump
- 2 - 3 run-bys over each jump
- Explain how to progress
- Options for practicing at home

Sample Course Outline
Beginning Agility — Week 3

Set-Up

SIDE 1	SIDE 2
<ul><li>Beginner weave poles</li><li>Standard weave poles</li><li>See-saw</li><li>Pause box</li><li>Collapsed tunnel (for practice)</li><li>Tire jump (for practice)</li><li>Pause table (for practice)</li><li>Pipe tunnel (for practice)</li><li>Tire jump (for practice)</li></ul>	<ul><li>A-frame (flattened to 5 1/2 ft.)</li><li>Cross-Over</li><li>Dog walk</li><li>Double bar and spread bar jumps in sequence, positioned 20 ft. apart</li><li>SIngle winged jumps (bar, barrel, bone - for practice)</li><li>Wingless jumps (high jump, bar jump, long jump - for practice)</li></ul>

INSTRUCTOR #1	INSTRUCTOR #2
Beginner and Standard Weave Poles <ul><li>Review method</li><li>1 time through beginner set, each dog for review</li><li>2 - 3 times through standard set</li></ul>**See-Saw** <ul><li>Explain rules</li><li>Possible commands</li><li>Explain/demo method</li><li>3 - 4 times each dog</li><li>Explain how to progress</li></ul>**Pause Box** <ul><li>Explain rules</li><li>Possible commands</li><li>Explain/demo method</li><li>3 - 4 times each dog</li><li>Explain how to progress</li><li>Options for practicing at home</li></ul>	**A-Frame (at 5 1/2 feet)** <ul><li>3 times each dog</li></ul>**Cross-Over** <ul><li>Explain/demo method for turns</li><li>1 - 2 right turns each dog</li><li>1 - 2 left turns each dog</li></ul>**Dog Walk** <ul><li>Explain rules</li><li>Possible commands</li><li>Explain/demo method</li><li>3 times each dog</li></ul>**Double and Spread Bar Jumps** <ul><li>Explain rules</li><li>1 - 2 recalls over each jump</li><li>2 - 3 run-bys over each jump</li><li>Explain how to progress</li><li>Options for practicing at home</li></ul>

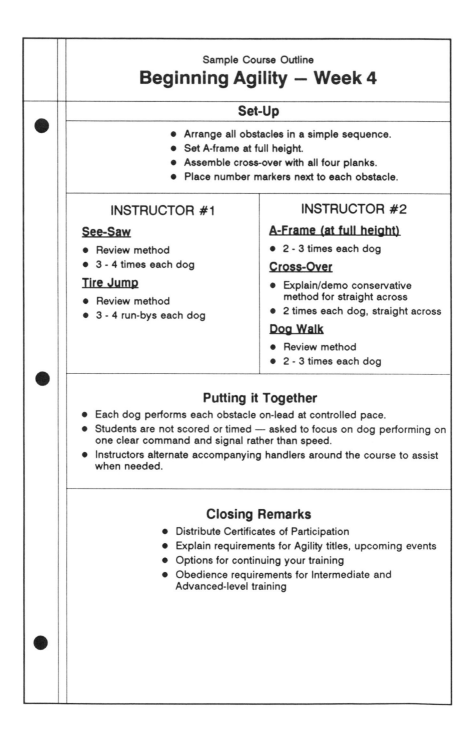

Sample Course Outline

Beginning Agility — Week 4

Set-Up

- Arrange all obstacles in a simple sequence.
- Set A-frame at full height.
- Assemble cross-over with all four planks.
- Place number markers next to each obstacle.

INSTRUCTOR #1

See-Saw

- Review method
- 3 - 4 times each dog

Tire Jump

- Review method
- 3 - 4 run-bys each dog

INSTRUCTOR #2

A-Frame (at full height)

- 2 - 3 times each dog

Cross-Over

- Explain/demo conservative method for straight across
- 2 times each dog, straight across

Dog Walk

- Review method
- 2 - 3 times each dog

Putting it Together

- Each dog performs each obstacle on-lead at controlled pace.
- Students are not scored or timed — asked to focus on dog performing on one clear command and signal rather than speed.
- Instructors alternate accompanying handlers around the course to assist when needed.

Closing Remarks

- Distribute Certificates of Participation
- Explain requirements for Agility titles, upcoming events
- Options for continuing your training
- Obedience requirements for Intermediate and Advanced-level training

each instructor teaches half of the obstacles that are covered in each class. Students are split into two groups, usually divided by jump height, and begin each session with one of the two instructors. At "half time" the students switch to the second instructor and remaining obstacles and complete the session. The advantages to this approach include consistency of instruction (since each obstacle is taught by only one instructor) and ease of preparation.

At the end of the fourth week, students perform each of the obstacles on-lead in a simple sequence with hurdles set at low height. Forget about speed and define success as getting dogs to perform each obstacle on one clear command and signal. An instructor accompanies each student around the course to provide spotting and assistance when needed. The purpose of this exercise is to provide a culminating experience for the students' four weeks of training.

A sample course outline for a Beginning Agility course is provided in the diagrams on the following pages. When the outline directs the instructor to "explain/demo method," the method is that described in chapter 3, Obstacle Training.

INTERMEDIATE AGILITY

Since many of those who enroll in Beginning Agility will want to continue their training past the "individual obstacle on-lead" level, you will need to provide additional training. Offer an intermediate-level class that focuses on developing a reliable performance on the obstacles, working toward full-height jumping and learning to sequence using various obstacle combinations. Dogs and handlers learn to negotiate two- and three-obstacle sequences using obstacles arranged in straight lines, right turns and left turns. Prerequisites for this class include the ability to guide the dog over each of the obstacles on-lead and some basic obedience training. The dog must sit, stay, down and come on command, regardless of distractions.

In Intermediate Agility, you may assume that those who enroll are interested in competition. Therefore encourage students to correct their dogs for sniffing or urinating while under a command, and for deliberately ignoring basic obedience commands. Strongly encourage students to obtain a set of weave poles and a set of hurdles for additional practice at home. The hurdles can be a manufactured set of obedience jumps (bar jump, high jump and broad jump) as described in chapter 3, Obstacle Training, or inexpensive homemade hurdles as described in chapter 10, Just for the Fun of It.

Intermediate class follows the same format as the Beginner course—four weeks duration, one hour per week, ten students and two instructors. During class it usually becomes obvious that some dogs do not respond reliably to the come command—the most essential command for Agility. In these cases, handlers are asked to place their dogs back on-lead and to work on the come command at home. These students then continue the four weeks on-lead, and should reenroll

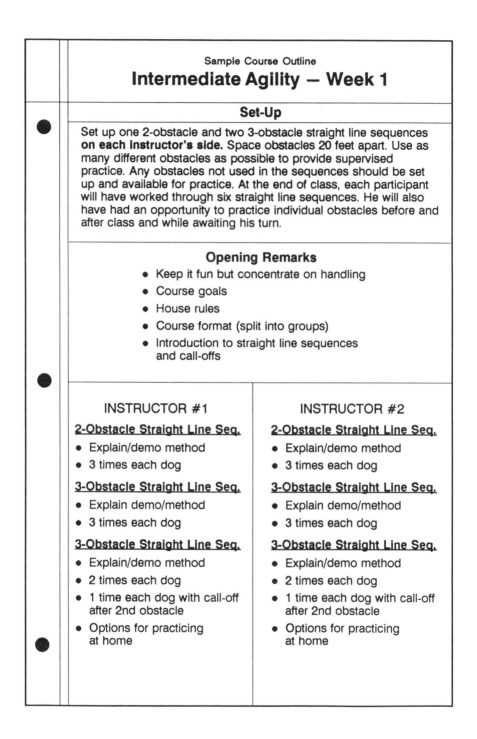

Sample Course Outline
Intermediate Agility — Week 1

Set-Up

Set up one 2-obstacle and two 3-obstacle straight line sequences **on each instructor's side.** Space obstacles 20 feet apart. Use as many different obstacles as possible to provide supervised practice. Any obstacles not used in the sequences should be set up and available for practice. At the end of class, each participant will have worked through six straight line sequences. He will also have had an opportunity to practice individual obstacles before and after class and while awaiting his turn.

Opening Remarks

- Keep it fun but concentrate on handling
- Course goals
- House rules
- Course format (split into groups)
- Introduction to straight line sequences and call-offs

INSTRUCTOR #1	INSTRUCTOR #2
2-Obstacle Straight Line Seq.	**2-Obstacle Straight Line Seq.**
• Explain/demo method	• Explain/demo method
• 3 times each dog	• 3 times each dog
3-Obstacle Straight Line Seq.	**3-Obstacle Straight Line Seq.**
• Explain demo/method	• Explain demo/method
• 3 times each dog	• 3 times each dog
3-Obstacle Straight Line Seq.	**3-Obstacle Straight Line Seq.**
• Explain/demo method	• Explain/demo method
• 2 times each dog	• 2 times each dog
• 1 time each dog with call-off after 2nd obstacle	• 1 time each dog with call-off after 2nd obstacle
• Options for practicing at home	• Options for practicing at home

Intermediate Agility — Week 2

Set-Up

Set up one 2-obstacle and two 3-obstacle right turn sequences **on each instructor's side.** Space obstacles 20 feet apart. Use as many different obstacles as possible to provide supervised practice. Any obstacles not used in the sequences should be set up and available for practice. At the end of class, each participant will have worked through six right turn sequences. He will also have had an opportunity to practice individual obstacles before and after class and while awaiting his turn.

Opening Remarks

- Review straight line sequences
- Introduction to right turn sequences handled off the left

INSTRUCTOR #1	INSTRUCTOR #2
2-Obstacle Right Turn Seq.	**2-Obstacle Right Turn Seq.**
• Explain/demo method	• Explain/demo method
• 3 times each dog	• 3 times each dog
3-Obstacle Right Turn Seq.	**3-Obstacle Right Turn Seq.**
• Explain demo/method	• Explain demo/method
• 3 times each dog	• 3 times each dog
3-Obstacle Right Turn Seq.	**3-Obstacle Right Turn Seq.**
• Explain/demo method	• Explain/demo method
• 2 times each dog	• 2 times each dog
• 1 time each dog with call-off after 2nd obstacle	• 1 time each dog with call-off after 2nd obstacle
• Options for practicing at home	• Options for practicing at home

Sample Course Outline
Intermediate Agility — Week 3

Set-Up

Set up one 2-obstacle and two 3-obstacle left turn sequences **on each instructor's side.** Space obstacles 20 feet apart. Use as many different obstacles as possible to provide supervised practice. Any obstacles not used in the sequences should be set up and available for practice. At the end of class each participant will have worked through six left turn sequences. He will also have had an opportunity to practice individual obstacles before and after class and while awaiting his turn.

Opening Remarks

- Review straight line and right turn sequences
- Introduction to left turn sequences handled off the right

INSTRUCTOR #1	INSTRUCTOR #2
2-Obstacle Left Turn Seq.	**2-Obstacle Left Turn Seq.**
• Explain/demo method	• Explain/demo method
• 3 times each dog	• 3 times each dog
3-Obstacle Left Turn Seq.	**3-Obstacle Left Turn Seq.**
• Explain demo/method	• Explain demo/method
• 3 times each dog	• 3 times each dog
3-Obstacle Left Turn Seq.	**3-Obstacle Left Turn Seq.**
• Explain/demo method	• Explain/demo method
• 2 times each dog	• 2 times each dog
• 1 time each dog with call-off after 2nd obstacle	• 1 time each dog with call-off after 2nd obstacle
• Options for practicing at home	• Options for practicing at home

Intermediate Agility — Week 4

Set-Up

Arrange all obstacles in a short course without traps, and with obstacles each taken only once. Place number markers and Start and Finish markers as appropriate.

INSTRUCTORS #1 and #2

- Allow students to practice individual obstacles or segments of the course for 15 minutes. Provide individual help as needed.
- Explain/demo judge's briefing and strategies for walking the course.
- Allow students to walk the course for 5 minutes.
- Have each student run the course off-lead, while instructor evaluates his progress

Closing Remarks

- Distribute Certificates of Participation
- Options for continuing your training

in Intermediate once they have mastered the recall. As in the Beginner class, use a station approach with five students per instructor. For safety reasons participants are asked to keep their dogs on-lead whenever they are not working.

Week one focuses on straight line sequences, week two, on right turns handling off the left and week three, on left turns handling off the right. Each week the student does three sequences with each instructor, for a total of six two- or three-obstacle sequences per class session. To give students the supervised experience they need on each obstacle and to provide practice in sequencing, try to include as many different obstacles as possible each night. When working with more than one difficult obstacle (weave poles, dog walk, crossover, see-saw and tire jump) in a sequence, restrict the sequence to only two obstacles.

At the beginning of week four, students may arrive at class to find a simple numbered course arranged. For the first fifteen minutes they warm up their dogs and may practice segments of the course or receive individual attention for any problems they are having. Discuss the "judge's briefing" that exhibitors receive before competing, and demonstrate how to "walk the course." Finally, students walk the course for themselves and run it with their dogs off-lead.

The instructors evaluate the students as to their ability to continue with advanced training. Students whose dogs do not respond to the recall reliably are asked to pursue more Obedience training and then reenroll in another intermediate-level class. As with dogs that need work on their recalls, dogs with obstacle problems must reenroll in Intermediate if their handlers want to continue with Agility training. All students, regardless of proficiency level, receive Certificates of Participation as a tribute to the accomplishments they have made with their dogs.

A sample course outline for an Intermediate Agility class is provided in the diagrams on the following pages. The size of your training area and type and quantity of available obstacles will help you determine what sequences to set up for each session. When the outline directs the instructor to "explain/demo method," the method is that described in the chapter 5, Sequence Training.

ADVANCED AGILITY

The greatest fun and challenge for both dogs and handlers comes through advanced-level training. Designed to prepare handlers for competition, advanced classes usually run continuously, with no set beginning or ending date.

Each session consists of an hour of class, followed by a half hour of open practice and individual attention. Classes alternate weekly between two formats: handling exercises and mock competitions. Exercises concentrate on advanced handling techniques, control at a distance, negotiating traps, improving speed and accuracy and developing ring strategies. On alternate weeks students gain experience by running a regulation Agility course (Standard, Jumpers, Pairs,

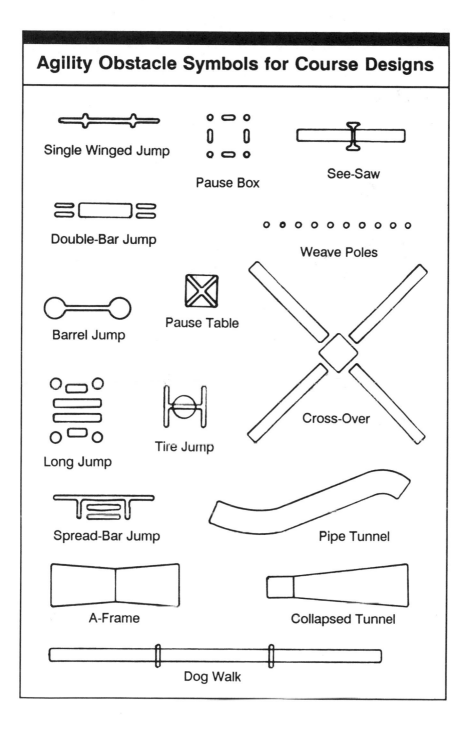

Agility Obstacle Symbols for Course Designs

Single Winged Jump

Pause Box

See-Saw

Double-Bar Jump

Weave Poles

Barrel Jump

Pause Table

Cross-Over

Long Jump

Tire Jump

Spread-Bar Jump

Pipe Tunnel

A-Frame

Collapsed Tunnel

Dog Walk

Gamblers or Snooker) while being judged and timed. Design the course layouts to work out problems in specific areas of difficulty. This allows students to put to use the skills learned during "handling exercise" weeks and offers students an opportunity to assess their own progress. After running the course and receiving suggestions from the instructor and other students, they run it once again to implement changes to their handling strategies. Advanced class prerequisites include the dog's ability to perform all obstacles off-lead and reliable responses to the sit, stay, down and come commands.

Advanced Class Exercises

Because the advanced classes contain students with varying levels of proficiency, design the exercises to be easily modified for different experience levels. Record the exercises and their variations (as well as the date last used) on index cards and store them in a card file by category. To determine which exercises to use for a particular class and day, look at the list of students who will be attending and select exercises to address their needs. The following pages provide a few sample ideas and guidelines for developing your own exercises. Once you begin holding advanced-level classes, it will become easier for you to create new exercises on your own.

Gambles (see also Chapter 8)

Nothing can match the feeling of pride you will have when your dog performs a difficult gamble sequence on its own. For this reason training gambles is one of the most pleasurable aspects of Advanced Agility training. Here are some suggestions for practicing gambles in your classes:

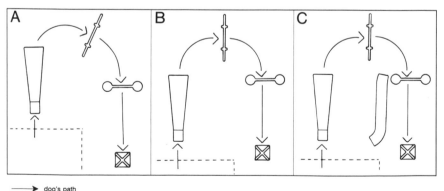

→ dog's path
handler remains behind dashed lines

Making a gamble more difficult.

- Use your creativity to set up challenging gambles that can be modified for different skill levels. For example, you can have beginners perform only the last two obstacles of the gamble. The reason you should practice extremely difficult gambles is not that you should expect to encounter them in competition (although, who knows?) but to ensure your dog's understanding of commands under the most difficult of circumstances. If your dog can perform the most challenging of gambles, it won't be fazed when presented with simpler ones—even with the excitement and distractions of an Agility trial.
- Practice gamble call-offs as described in chapter 6, Distance Control, varying the point at which the handler calls the dog off. Also try different types of call-offs—calling the dog back over a previous obstacle or straight to the handler without taking obstacles.

Distance Control

In addition to practicing gambles, here are a few suggestions for exercises in distance control:

- Practice signal and command recognition by positioning the dog between two obstacles and commanding or signaling to one or the other (as described in chapter 6, Distance Control).
- Proof the dog's recognition of verbal commands by positioning beside the handler, equidistant from two side-by-side obstacles, and commanding to one or the other (as described in chapter 6, Distance Control).
- Practice sending the dog over a hurdle, then commanding left or right and sending over another hurdle. Use low jump heights for beginners and higher ones for more accomplished dogs. This exercise is only for those handlers who have already trained left and right. For those who haven't, demonstrate techniques for training left and right to be practiced at home as an obedience command.
- Set up sequences to practice in which a go-out command is followed by a command to turn left or right, using the procedures described in chapter 6, Distance Control.
- Have handlers send their dogs over a hurdle to a table positioned 25 to 30 feet away. Challenge advanced handlers to send their dogs from a standstill, while allowing beginners a running start.
- Mark a 10-foot-wide square on the ground as a starting point for dog and handler. (A circle would work just as well but it is easier to mark off a square.) Position the pause table, pause box, pipe tunnel, tire jump and a single-type hurdle around and about 15 feet from the edges of the square. The object is to send the dog to each of the five obstacles without the handler leaving the square. For advanced dogs, make the square progressively smaller so that the handler is ultimately sending the dog

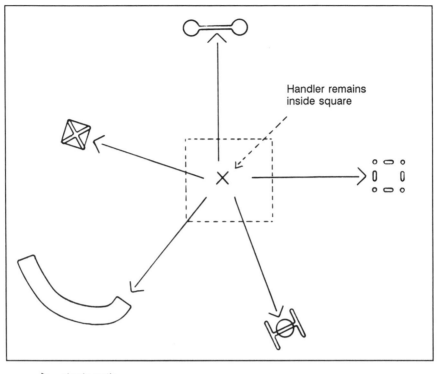

Handler remains
inside square

→ dog's path

Distance control exercise.

from a standstill. For a greater challenge, send advanced dogs through/
over one obstacle to another, such as through the tunnel to the pause
table.

- Set up a straight line sequence of three hurdles followed by a finish line.
  Practice sending the dogs over the hurdles and then over the finish line
  with the go-out command, using the methods described in chapter 6,
  Distance Control. For those who have not trained the go-out, demonstrate
  techniques for training the command to be practiced at home in a setting
  separate from Agility class.
- Capitalize on the competitive nature of many Agility enthusiasts by
  seeing who can send his or her dog the farthest to the pause table, pause
  box or one of the tunnels. For advanced dogs, practice sending them to
  the tunnels at an angle.
- Have handlers practice getting a head start while their dogs are in a
  down-stay on the pause table. Set up a series of obstacles beginning
  with a pause table and have the handlers call the dogs over/through one
  or more obstacles, depending on their experience levels.

Right- and Left-Side Handling

The ability to handle equally well off your right and your left is a great advantage in the Agility ring. The following are suggestions for exercises in switching sides and handling off either side:

- Set up simple straight line sequences using a variety of obstacles. Depending upon the speed of the dog and the obstacles used, practice switching sides both ahead of and behind the dog. Vary the point at which the handler switches sides.
- Practice switching sides while making turns during jump sequences. Practice using both the "fake-out" technique and the "send-away" technique (chapter 5). For beginning dogs, use single-type hurdles; for more experienced dogs, use spread-type hurdles.
- Set up right and left turn sequences incorporating obstacles other than hurdles and practice switching sides.
- Set up a five- or six-obstacle sequence (beginning with a hurdle) to be handled entirely off the right. For beginning dogs, use only two or three of the obstacles.

Reliability

Some dogs have little trouble performing Agility on their own training ground, but succumb to the distractions of a new location or equipment. Here are a few ideas for increasing the dogs' reliability under a variety of circumstances:

- Proof against "scavenging" by deliberately littering the ground with objects to entice your dog to investigate or sniff while working. Vary the degree of temptation according to the dogs' level of experience and previous proofing: Use benign scraps of paper for beginners, empty food wrappers for more experienced dogs and actual pieces of food, tennis balls or toys for the ultimate distractions. Handlers should work with their dogs on-lead or with a tab and be ready to apply a timely correction, if needed.
- Take a "field trip" and move some of your obstacles to a new training location—especially to a noisy public area with an abundance of strange sights, smells and sounds.
- Arrange a "swap" with another Agility training group in which you practice on their equipment and they practice on yours.
- Proof the dogs to ignore noise distractions by having classmates clap and cheer while the dogs are working. For more experienced dogs, play tape recordings of loud music, strange noises and dog show sounds.
- Proof the dogs to ignore extraneous people on the course (such as judges, timekeepers, stewards and scribes) by having other students (or strangers,

if possible) mill about while they are performing exercises and running courses.

- Disguise your hurdles and other obstacles occasionally to make them appear unfamiliar-looking to the dogs.

Traps

As in training for gambles, it pays to set up extremely challenging traps to prepare your dog to perform simpler ones while under the stress of competition. Here are some suggestions for practicing traps:

- Arrange difficult sequences with an incorrect obstacle placed directly in the dog's path. With experienced dogs, position traps 15 feet or closer to the correct path. With less experienced dogs, position the traps farther away.
- Practice traps involving two obstacles with different names that are positioned close to one another. Proof the dogs' recognition of obstacle names by sending them to one or the other as described in chapter 6, Distance Control. Using the same setup, practice avoiding the traps through approach and handler body positioning rather than by the dogs' discrimination of voice commands. Also, practice switching sides when approaching a trap to block the dog's view of the incorrect obstacle.

Jump Sequences

Even the most experienced dogs and handlers make timing mistakes or poor approaches to hurdles while in the throes of a fast-paced jump sequence. Since hurdles make up such a large percentage of the obstacles on an Agility course, it pays to devote ample attention to practicing jump sequences. Some examples follow:

- Arrange four hurdles in a circle at right angles to one another, 15 to 20 feet apart. Practice clockwise and counterclockwise circles, jumping all four hurdles. Then call off after three; then about-turn after two; then call off after one, etc.
- Work on sharp right and left turns using two spread-type hurdles such as the long jump and the spread-bar jump. Use wider (20-foot) spacing for beginning dogs and tighter spacing for more advanced ones.
- Use your imagination to create as many challenging jump sequences as possible, incorporating sharp turns, intentional back-jumping, tight spacing, send-aways, directional control and side switching. Ruth Hobday's book *Agility Is Fun!* (see reference in Appendix B) contains several excellent examples of jump sequence exercises that can get you started.
- Practice jump sequences with offset and angled jumps.

Weave Poles

By the time students reach advanced-level classes, there is still much the dogs must learn in order to reach their potential in performing the weave poles. Below are some ideas for exercises:

- Work on reliably handling the weave poles off the right.
- Practice approaching the weave poles after a sharp left turn to ensure that the dog knows to enter from the right.
- Work on both calling the dog through and sending the dog through the weave poles. Use one set of poles for beginners and two sets combined for advanced dogs. Practice sending advanced dogs through the weave poles from various angles.
- Set up a fast-paced jumping sequence concluding with the weave poles. Practice the approach to the poles by holding the dog back and controlling the entry. With advanced dogs, practice sending the dog ahead to enter on its own without slowing down.
- After performing the weave poles in one direction, make a tight about-turn and perform them again in the opposite direction. Handlers often waste precious time with sloppy turns when making this maneuver. Practice with one five-pole set as well as with both sets put together. The exit direction is different in each case, which affects the handler's footwork for the about-turn.
- Work on increasing the dogs' speed through the weave poles, using food, toys and/or enthusiastic cheering.

Miscellaneous

The following are a few ideas for exercises that don't neatly fit into one of the other categories:

- Work on increasing the speed through individual obstacles and short sequences using motivational techniques and selectively rewarding the dog for faster speeds. Have someone use a stopwatch to time the dogs and make note of their improvement.
- Practice quick, enthusiastic "starts." Beginners can call their dogs over one hurdle, while the more advanced students can call their dogs over three or more obstacles. Motivate using an excited tone of voice, re strained recalls or food or toy rewards as the dog reaches the handler. For experienced dogs, add cheering and other distractions to simulate the stress of a competition start.
- Pattern the dogs to touch the contact zones by setting up fast approaches or sharp-angle approaches to contact obstacles. Use hoops or handling techniques (described in chapter 3, Obstacle Training) to address any problems.

- Set up a sequence of obstacles and have dogs perform the entire sequence. Then repeat the sequence, the second time performing only selected obstacles while bypassing the others. Keep the dog guessing and attentive by performing several variations using the same set-up, bypassing different obstacles each time.
- Work on the again command using hurdles. For beginners, use a single-type hurdle and run alongside the dog; for the most advanced, use spread-type hurdles and send the dogs over and back at a distance. Alternate between asking the dog to back-jump using "Again," and calling the dog around the hurdle without allowing to jump. Also practice "Again" using obstacles other than hurdles.
- Set up a Snooker course and practice only the opening sequence. When setting up the course, include many well-placed traps among the obstacles. Discuss handling options and strategies and try them.
- Set up a Gamblers course without the gamble and practice different strategies for accumulating points.
- Practice baton hand-offs for the Pairs Relay class.

DESIGNING AGILITY COURSES

When designing courses, the arrangements are left mainly to your imagination, although the *Official Rules and Regulations of the United States Dog Agility Association* provide a few guidelines to follow.

Each type of competition class has different criteria for course design. To help you design courses for advanced classes, here are some guidelines for each type of class. Some are based on regulations as of this writing, while some are practical considerations, based on my experiences as an Agility judge, that are not yet addressed in the *Official Rules*.

Standard Classes

When creating course designs for Standard classes, keep the following in mind:

- Place obstacles approximately 15 feet apart.
- If a hurdle will be used twice in a row (intentional back-jumping) or soon enough so that a steward will not have enough time to replace a knocked-down bar or board, avoid using hurdles such as the double-bar jump. These hurdles are common targets of knock-downs and the bars are time-consuming to replace. Consider using the tire jump, long jump or a single-type hurdle instead. If the steward does not have enough time to replace the knocked down bar or board before the dog repeats the hurdle, the dog incurs "double jeopardy"—it must receive a penalty

for displacing the bar the second time since the dog did not have the opportunity to jump it at full height.

- The spread-bar jump and see-saw are designed to be used in only one direction. Other hurdles, such as many varieties of the bone jump, are also one-way hurdles because the bar or board is only displaceable in one direction.
- Plan the course so that the judge has to do a minimum amount of running to be in a position to judge the performance of contact zones, weave poles and the pause obstacles. The judge should not be expected to run the entire length of the course for each dog.
- Although it is not a written rule, it adds excitement to end the course with a fast-moving jump sequence.
- Use between eleven and twenty obstacles. The more obstacles you use, the faster the course times the dogs will achieve because of the higher ratio of hurdles to other more time-consuming obstacles.
- The course must include three or four contact obstacles (one may be used twice), pipe tunnel, collapsed tunnel, pause table or pause box (but not both), weave poles, tire jump and three hurdles, one of which must be a spread-type hurdle.
- Incorporate at least one or more traps in each course. Make the traps more difficult to avoid for the Advanced and Master's level courses.
- Include sequences that are most efficiently handled off the right as well as those best handled off the left.
- For spectator appeal, try to design a course that flows smoothly, while still incorporating several sharp changes in direction and tight turns.
- Do your best to balance your course design to be as fair as possible to all sizes of dogs. Long, smooth-flowing courses with wide obstacle spacing favor large dogs, while shorter courses with tight spacing and sharp turns favor small dogs. Large dogs benefit from courses that include many hurdles in a row, while small dogs are more competitive with course designs that break up hurdle sequences with contact obstacles. This is because large-dog handlers must slow down their dogs for each approach to a contact obstacle, while small-dog handlers need not.

The diagram on page 146 shows an example of a Standard course. With an eighteen-obstacle layout, it is a smooth-flowing course that provides numerous traps, handle-off-the-right as well as handle-off-the-left sequences and several 90-degree turns.

Gamblers Courses (see also Chapter 8)

Since Gamblers is a Non-Standard class, much of the course design and judging criteria are flexible and left up to you. When Gamblers or any other Non-Standard class is used as a titling class for Masters-level certification, how-

Standard Course Design Example

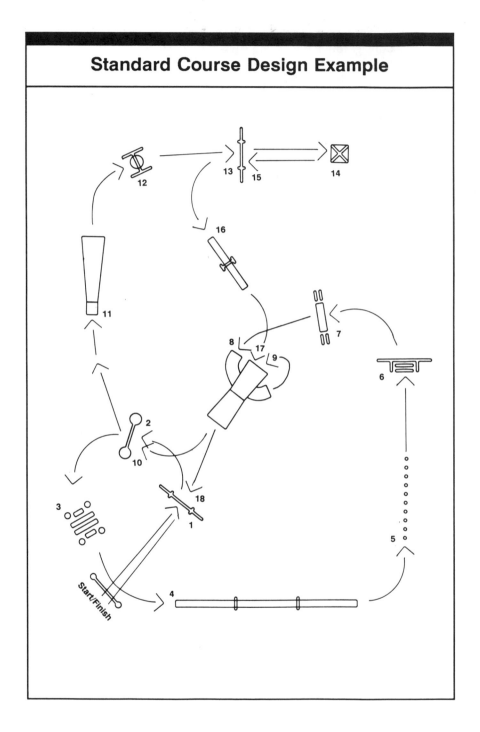

Gamblers Course Design Example

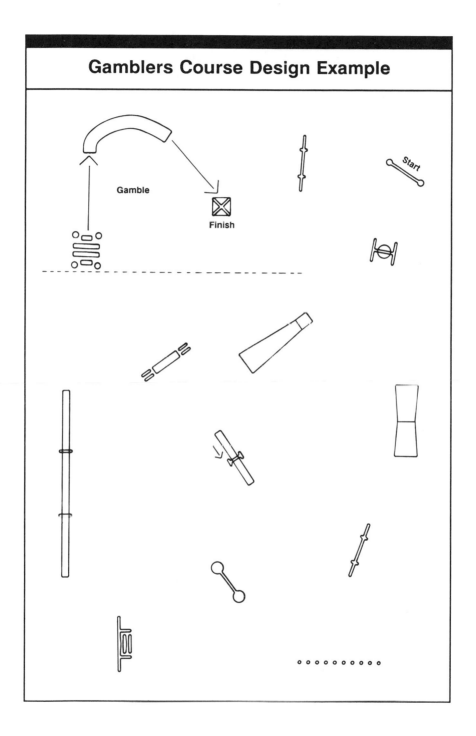

ever, certain requirements (which are specified in the *Official Rules*) must be met. Here are some general guidelines for designing Gamblers courses:

- The same minimum obstacle requirements apply to Gamblers as apply to Standard courses, except that the pause table (or pause box) can be used as a start or finish line, or not at all.
- Assign point values to the obstacles according to one of the point systems outlined in the *Official Rules*.
- Position high-value obstacles away from one another and away from the gamble.
- Most judges allow ten to fifteen seconds for the gamble, assign ten to twenty bonus points for successful completion and deduct five to fifteen points for failed attempts. The easier the gamble, the less time you should allow for its completion and the fewer points you should award for successful performance. Assign more time and more points to more difficult gambles. Also, the more difficult a gamble, the smaller your penalty should be for failed attempts. This encourages handlers to try the gamble, which adds to the fun and excitement of the class.
- Make sure there is more than one attractive option for choosing a course path.
- If possible, don't use one-way hurdles (hurdles that have bars or boards that are only displaceable in one direction). If you do, it's up to the judge whether these may be taken in either direction.

In Gamblers, it is a common practice for the judge to tell handlers when they have missed a contact zone. As soon as the fault is committed, the judge calls out "Fault!" or "Missed it!" so that handlers know they may attempt the obstacle again. During the judge's briefing, the judge should tell exhibitors how (or if) he or she intends to call out faults.

An example of a Gamblers course design is shown in the diagram on page 147. Notice that the weave poles, which are usually assigned the highest point value, are located far from both the start line and the gamble. The contact obstacles, which are also assigned high point values, are distributed throughout the course. When attempting the gamble, the handler must stay behind the dotted line while the dog performs the sequence. If the handler chooses to go to the finish line and skip the gamble, she can ignore the line and go to the table with her dog.

Snooker Courses (see also Chapter 8)

Follow these guidelines when designing Snooker courses:

- Make sure there is more than one attractive option for choosing obstacles in the opening sequence.
- Include several well-placed traps.

Snooker Course Design Example

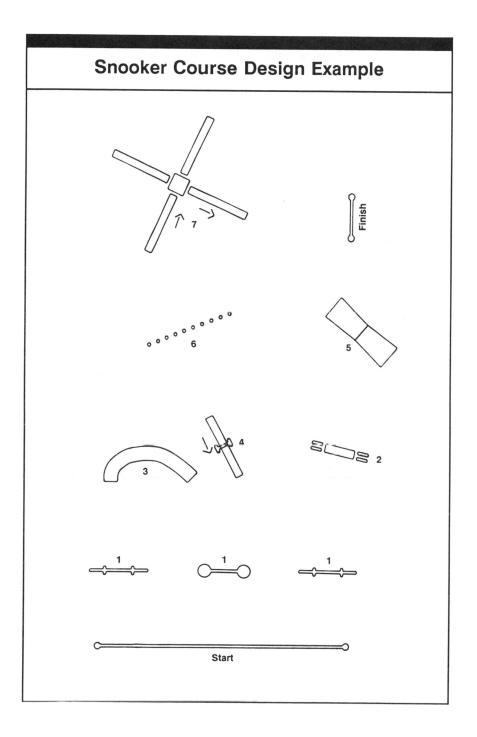

- Try to make it possible for the fastest, most well-controlled dogs to make it to the highest-value obstacles in the opening sequence and still have just enough time to complete the closing sequence.
- Position the obstacles so that the higher the point value, the more difficult and time-consuming it is to perform during the opening sequence. There needs to be an element of risk involved; otherwise, everyone will head directly for the high-value obstacles.

The diagram on page 149 shows a sample Snooker course design. To start, handlers may position their dogs anywhere behind the start line. Although none are provided in this example, you can include extra obstacles that carry no point values and act as "traps" around the course. This makes for an even more interesting competition!

Jumpers Courses (see also Chapter 8)

Often the most limiting factor in designing Jumpers courses is the number of available hurdles. When equipment is limited, course designers must be more creative and use existing hurdles two or three times each. Here are some guidelines for designing Jumpers courses:

- Include a number of difficult maneuvers and set up some sequences that require handling off the right as well as some that are best handled off the left. Too simple a course yields a plethora of boring, "clear" rounds in which speed alone determines the winner.
- Use between twelve and twenty hurdles, counting those that are taken more than once. For example, if your group has only eight hurdles, your course design must use four of the hurdles twice to achieve the twelve-hurdle minimum.
- Your course design must incorporate at least three spread-type hurdles (such as the long jump, double-bar jump and spread-bar jump).
- If a hurdle will be jumped twice in a row (intentional back-jumping) or soon enough so that a steward will not have enough time to replace a knocked-down bar or board, consider using the tire jump, long jump or a single-type jump instead, for the same reasons as specified for standard courses.
- Position one-way hurdles so that they will be jumped in one direction only.

An example of a Jumpers course design is provided on page 152. This course includes sixteen obstacles using only eight different hurdles. To provide a challenge to handlers, the course requires handling off the right as well as handling off the left, several 90-degree turns and an intentional back-jump.

Pairs Relay Courses (see also Chapter 8)

The following guidelines apply to designing Pairs Relay courses:

- Most guidelines for standard courses are applicable, except that the Pairs Relay course should have at least eleven obstacles, with each dog performing at least five obstacles. The pause obstacles are not required and are rarely used in the Pairs Relay class (except as start and finish positions). The contact obstacles are also not required but are normally used to add variety and challenge.
- You can design a more interesting course if you specify that both dogs in the pair must share the same jump height. That way you can use hurdles more than once in the course. If you accept pairs of mixed jump heights, you must work harder (and have more hurdles available) to design an interesting course. Otherwise, it often becomes a large, boring circle with each dog performing half the circle.
- Your baton-handoff area can be inside a designated location such as a box or behind a line.
- Try to balance the course so that each dog's portion is equally challenging.

The diagram on page 153 shows an example of a Pairs Relay course. It was designed to accommodate pairs with different jump heights, since this is the more difficult course to create. The course begins with the first dog on the pause table, while the second dog and handler wait inside the pause box. The first dog completes obstacles one through nine and returns to the pause table, while his handler passes the baton to the second handler (who must be inside the box with his dog during the hand-off). This example is a fairly balanced course since both dogs perform all the contact obstacles, both tunnels, three hurdles and the weave poles. The first dog encounters an extra trap and the second dog performs an extra obstacle.

Measuring Courses (see also Chapter 8)

For classes that require the dog to be judged against a Standard Course Time (such as Standard classes and Jumpers), you need to determine the length of the course. Although you can get a rough idea of the course length from your course diagram, to get an accurate figure you need to measure the actual course after the obstacles are in place.

Pace off a course by starting at the start line and ending at the finish line, taking a path for the average dog, being sure to give adequate room to approach the obstacles. To take an accurate path, step over the hurdles, if possible. For any obstacles you cannot step over, step around them, but do not always take

Jumpers Course Design Example

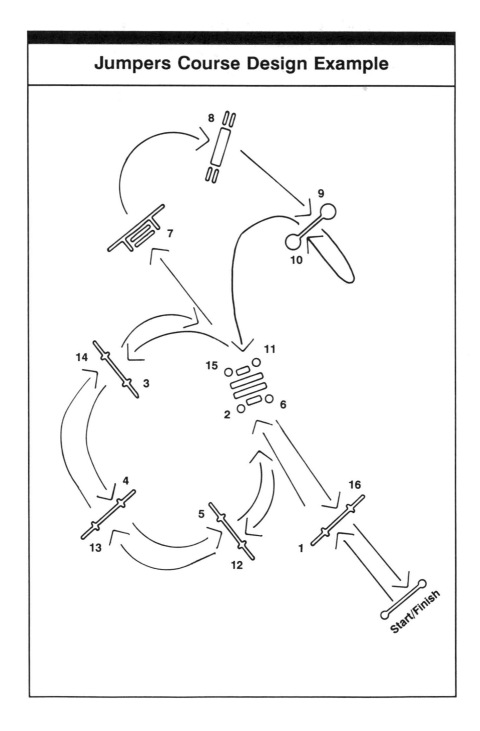

Pairs Relay Course Design Example

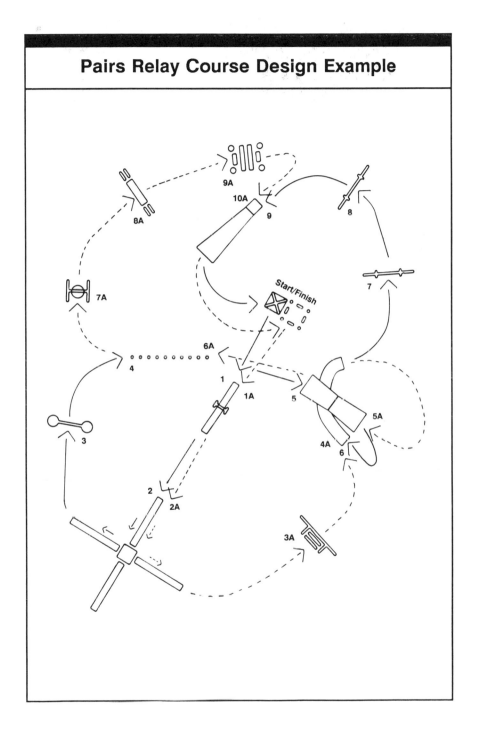

153

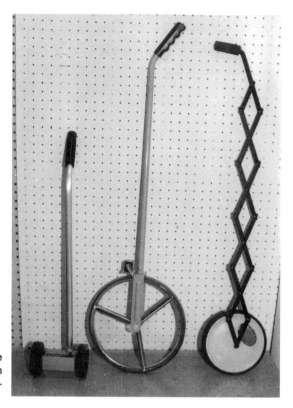

Surveyors' measuring wheels are useful for measuring the length of a course quickly and accurately.

the shortest path. Instead, balance your measurement by half the time walking around the outside of the obstacle and the other half of the time walking around the inside. Multiply your total number of paces by the length of your stride in yards to determine the course length. If your stride tends to vary, or if you want to be absolutely sure of your measurement, you may find it useful to use a surveyor's measuring wheel to measure off the length of the course. These come in various shapes and sizes—some even fit inside a briefcase for travel.

To determine the Standard Course Time (SCT), divide the course length (in yards) by the constant used for the particular class. The current constant is 2 yards per second for the Starters class; other constants range upward for higher level classes. (These constants *do* change, so "constant" isn't a very appropriate term!) For a course length of 160 yards, a Starters SCT would be eighty seconds. Notice that no time is added for the five seconds the dog spends on the pause obstacle. This is already taken into account by the constant.

IN CONCLUSION

The hardest part of almost anything new is knowing where to begin. I hope this chapter has planted a few seeds for developing your own curriculum of training classes. Always keep in mind the goals of your students while teaching your classes, especially at the beginning level—the training is for them, not for you.

To determine the *actual* effectiveness, observe the dogs at the final session of each course. Have they met the stated course goals? If not, in what ways are their performances lacking? Deficiencies shared by many students should be suspect—how can you improve the course to help eradicate these problem areas? If deficiencies exist in *perceived* effectiveness, how can you make training more enjoyable and rewarding for students? As a result of your periodic "reality checks," your students will be happier and you will have good reason to be proud when they do well in the Agility ring!

Performing a difficult "gamble"—through the tire, through the weave poles and to the pause table, while the handler remains behind the tire jump.

8

Agility Trial Classes and Competition

WHEN YOU and your four-legged friend are reasonably good at running a course together, it's time to start considering entering competitive Agility events. There's no reason to wait until your performance is flawless— dogs and handlers at all levels of Agility training are entered in competition. Besides, early ring experience will help shape your future training by pointing out your dog's problem areas—for example, succumbing to distractions, lack of attention or insecurity on one or more of the obstacles. Above all, you'll have an enjoyable day's outing with your dog and with others who share your love of the sport.

Some Agility events allow you to enter "For Exhibition Only," which means you do not compete for prizes and your score does not count toward Agility titles. In return, you're given the freedom to break some of the competition rules, such as using a collar or lead, carrying food, toys or other inducements in the ring or jumping a lower height than your dog would normally be required to jump. Entering "For Exhibition Only" can be a great experience for the novice Agility dog that may be insecure in the ring. Different events offer varying degrees of latitude for people showing "For Exhibition Only." Check with the host organization for details about what you can and cannot do.

AGILITY TRIAL CLASSES

When you enter an Agility trial, you can normally choose from several events or "classes" being offered. Each class has different rules and requirements. Although some of the current rules are provided in this book, you will need to consult the *Official Rules and Regulations of the United States Dog Agility Association* (see Appendix B) for a complete set of up-to-date rules.

Because Agility is a rapidly evolving sport, the rules also evolve rapidly, especially as dogs and handlers become more skilled in the Agility ring. Two important rules that apply to all classes at official "sanctioned" trials (as opposed to informal practice "matches") are that your dog must perform without a leash or collar, and you may not carry food, toys or other inducements into the ring.

Agility trial classes are normally divided into Standard and Non-Standard classes.

Standard Classes

Standard classes include the sanctioned "titling" classes (in which dogs can earn Agility titles), such as Starters, Novice, Advanced and Masters, as well as other classes, such as Open, in which titles are not awarded. In Standard classes the course layout consists of eleven to twenty obstacles, which are sequentially numbered and must be taken in order.

Each course is assigned a Standard Course Time (SCT) based on the length of the course in yards. Dogs incur "time faults" for each second (or fraction thereof) the dog exceeds the SCT. For example, if a dog takes 95.6 seconds to complete a course with an SCT of 90 seconds, he incurs 5.6 time faults.

Dogs and handlers are also faulted for infractions they commit while running a course. These "course faults" are assessed for

- Failure to perform an obstacle
- Taking an obstacle out of sequence or in the wrong direction
- Knocking off a bar or board on a hurdle
- Sliding off the pause table or running out of the pause box
- Missing a contact zone

Faults may also be assessed if the handler touches the dog or an obstacle. At the higher levels of competition, dogs also receive course faults for any significant hesitation in response to a handler's command, called a "refusal." Each course infraction carries a five-fault penalty, with the exception of failure to perform an obstacle, which is a twenty-fault penalty for each occurrence.

A dog's time faults are added to course faults to determine total faults. The dog with the fewest total faults is the winner, and in the event of a tie, the winner is the dog with the fastest time.

At most competitions you will see the judge signal the occurrence of a fault by raising a hand at the moment of the infraction, so the audience knows immediately when a dog has incurred a fault. (The exhibitor is usually too busy watching the dog to see whether or not the judge raises a hand!) As the judge signals the faults, an assistant, called the "scribe," marks them on the dog's scoresheet. In the absence of a scribe, judges mark their own scoresheets instead of signaling faults.

To earn an Agility Dog^{SM} (AD) title, you need to complete one faultless (clear) round in the Starters or Novice class. The **Starters** class is for dogs that have not yet earned the AD title and are handled by a person who *has not* earned an Agility title with another dog. The **Novice** class is for dogs that have not yet earned the AD title and are handled by a person who *has* achieved an Agility title on another dog. The rules and course designs for the Starters and Novice classes are identical. The purpose behind offering two classes is to allow newcomers to the sport to compete only with other newcomers, thus affording them a better opportunity to earn placements and awards.

The **Advanced** class is for dogs that have earned an AD title and are working toward an Advanced Agility Dog^{SM} (AAD) title. To earn an AAD title, you need to earn three clear rounds under two different judges in the Advanced class. Compared to Starters and Novice, the Advanced class requires dogs to demonstrate higher performance standards, including greater handler control, working consistency and faster speeds.

After earning the AAD title, dogs can compete in the **Masters** class—an extremely fast-paced and challenging display of teamwork between dog and handler. To earn a Master Agility Dog^{SM} (MAD) title, you must earn a clear round in the Masters class and a qualifying score in each of the following:

- Gamblers class
- Pairs or Team class
- Your choice of another Non-Standard class, or another qualifying score in the Masters class under a different judge.

Non-Standard Classes

Non-Standard classes, also called Novelty classes, are usually offered along with Standard classes to provide diversity for both exhibitors and spectators.

In **Jumpers**, dogs traverse a fast-paced course consisting only of a variety of hurdles. Like regular classes, Jumpers is judged against a Standard Course Time and the dog with the fewest faults wins.

Gamblers is a fun class you can enter at almost any stage in your Agility training. The obstacles are arranged randomly on the course and you and your dog have a fixed amount of time to complete as many obstacles as possible in the given amount of time. Normally, you are permitted to take each obstacle a maximum of twice, in either direction. You receive more points for contact obstacles and fewer points for hurdles—the fun is in choosing your strategy!

At the end of the specified time period a whistle blows and you have a

A competitor running a difficult course at a national event.

choice: Take the points you have accumulated and call it quits by heading for the finish line, or try your luck at the "gamble." The gamble is a series of obstacles that your dog must complete in a very limited amount of time. The catch is that you must send the dog to perform the obstacles without your going along. A classic entry-level gamble requires you to send your dog through the tire jump, through a curved tunnel and onto the pause table without your stepping past the tire jump. Successfully completing the gamble rewards you with bonus points, which will often ensure you a place "in the ribbons." Failure results in a point-reduction penalty. The dog with the most points accumulated wins, and in the event of a tie, time determines the winner.

Snooker is an exciting class that combines all the best Agility has to offer—strategy, speed, control and teamwork. Although the rules are a bit complicated, once you have tried Snooker it is likely to become one of your favorite classes. Like Gamblers, the goal is to accumulate as many points as possible in a limited amount of time. Snooker begins with you and your dog completing an "opening sequence" consisting of three hurdles alternating with three obstacles of your own choosing. After you complete the opening sequence, you perform a "closing sequence" of six numbered obstacles with increasing point value, numbered "2" through "7" respectively. The dog accumulates points by completing the obstacles in sequence until the allotted time expires.

Any fault made during the closing sequence is met with the sound of a whistle, and the dog and handler then leave the ring with whatever points were accumulated prior to the whistle. The winner is the dog that accumulates the most points. For a complete description of the rules of Snooker, see the current *Official Rules and Regulations of the United States Dog Agility Association*.

In **Pairs Relay**, teams composed of two dogs and two handlers compete in a relay race. The first handler carries a baton and directs the dog to complete a designated section of a numbered course (or sometimes the entire course). They return to their finish line and the first handler passes the baton to the second handler, who then runs the second dog through the remaining section. A team's score is the total course time (for both dogs) and total course faults. The *lowest* score wins. Relay races can also be held for teams of three or more dogs.

Team competition typically consists of four people and four dogs, although the number can vary. Each dog completes a standard numbered course as if it were an individual competition. The total faults are added for each dog on the team and the team with the fewest faults wins. In case of a tie, the total time for all four dogs determines the winning team.

Tournaments

Tournaments are special Agility events, usually supported by a well-known sponsor. New rules may be established specifically for the tournament, and titling classes are usually not offered.

The Grand Prix of Dog Agility^{SM} has been a popular annual tournament, serving as the Agility national competition since 1988. Each year regional com-

The author at the 1990 USDAA National Finals Competition at the Grand Prix of Dog Agility^{SM}, Houston, Texas   *Photo: Gene Abrahamson*

petitions are held throughout the United States to determine who is eligible for the national semifinals. The tournament culminates in a thrilling finals competition, displaying the most outstanding Agility competitors the country has to offer. With each year the competitive level reaches a new peak, as more and more handlers are training at advanced levels.

TYPES OF COMPETITIONS

Upcoming Agility competitions are rarely announced in the local paper. Instead, show-sponsoring clubs advertise these events through dog-related publications and by mailing flyers to Agility training groups and known competitors. Once you start entering Agility events, you will most likely be placed on several mailing lists. Until then your best bet is to keep in contact with Agility training groups in your area.

Agility events come in a wide variety of forms. Also, the style of the equipment and the rules can vary, so before you decide to send in your entry fees or make a long trip, make sure the type of competition you are considering coincides with your Agility goals.

A "sanctioned" event will be identified as such in the event flyer or advertisement. These events are held under the published rules and regulations of an organization such as USDAA or NCDA and are judged by licensed judges. All obstacles used must be sturdy and conform to the organization's published specifications, so you should expect no surprises as far as the obstacles you will use in competition.

"Nonsanctioned" events cover a wide range of possibilities, the least formal of which is called a "match" or "fun match." It's usually inexpensive to enter a match, since the costs of holding matches are low. The match judge is usually a local Agility enthusiast, and the prizes are modest. A nonsanctioned event that is advertised as an "Agility Trial" probably differs from a match in that the entry fees are higher. Prizes may also be more generous, and rules may be less flexible. Nonsanctioned events can vary widely in the types of obstacles they use and the rules they follow for competition. Although most of these events are well run and provide safe conditions for dogs, some may include equipment that is wobbly or contact obstacles that are slippery. Attending nonsanctioned events can be great fun while providing valuable training experiences, as you are usually allowed to enter "For Exhibition Only."

Before traveling a great distance, research the conditions (if not specified in the ad) by calling the contact person listed on the event flyer. Ask about the jumping surface. Grass or packed dirt is best, while concrete should be avoided. Concrete surfaces can sometimes be slippery, and the impact from repeated jumping on concrete can be hard on the dog's joints. Even rough concrete can be hazardous since repeated jumping can injure the dogs' paw pads. Concrete flooring with padded rubber matting is acceptable, although it's rare to find an event with sufficient matting. Loose dirt can provide difficult footing for the dog, but it is preferable to concrete. Ask about the obstacles to determine whether they match those with which your dog is familiar—were they were built to Standard specifications? If so, which Standard? Which obstacles will be used? What rules will be followed?

Some events will require you to preenter, while some will accept entries at the door. In the latter case, you can often save a few dollars by preentering, since the day-of-show fees are usually higher.

BEFORE THE SHOW

Make sure your dog is clean and free of fleas. You'll understand why this is important when you live the horror of watching your dog stop to scratch an itch in the middle of your run as the precious seconds tick by. Also make sure your dog's nails are trimmed to a reasonably short length. Nails that are too long can cause traction problems on the contact obstacles and can be painful to the dog when climbing the A-frame.

Most outdoor Agility events are held regardless of weather, so plan to dress for any weather possibility. Dressing in layers is often a good idea.

Comfortable footwear with rubber soles and good tread are essential. A course can become very slippery from a sudden thunderstorm. One soggy competition, after watching handler after handler take a dive on a muddy course, I looked down at my treadless nonathletic shoes and knew I was in trouble. Luckily, the gate steward was wearing a pair of good-quality washable running shoes—in my size! Ever since then, washable running shoes are an integral part of my Agility trial attire.

Agility events are usually all-day affairs, so bring whatever you need to keep your dog and yourself comfortable. Depending upon the show site, this may include a lawn chair, water and a water bowl for your dog, food for both of you, sunscreen, insect repellent and perhaps a dog crate or exercise pen. Some people even bring a portable canopy (a tarp supported by poles and stakes) to protect them from the sun, rain or snow if shelter will be unavailable. Agility events are rarely canceled in bad weather because of the difficulty and expense of rescheduling and the indomitable spirit of Agility enthusiasts.

ARRIVAL AND WARM-UP

Plan to arrive at the show site well before the end of the scheduled check-in period. When you arrive at the show, check in at the registration table and pick up your armband. (The armband is printed with your entry number—you must wear it while you are in the ring.) This is the time to make sure your dog is entered in the right jump-height category and to inform the show personnel

Checking in at an Agility trial.

if you have decided to enter "For Exhibition Only" (if allowed). Ask when warm-ups will start and what the jump-height order will be. Then, if you haven't already done so, find a comfortable place to settle down with your dog and wait for your turn to warm up.

Sponsoring clubs are not required to provide warm-up sessions, but they usually do. Though it is often called warm-ups, the purpose is to familiarize your dog with a particular group's equipment. The group may use different-looking obstacles that conform to specifications but present an unfamiliar sight picture to the dog. The session is not intended as a warm-up for the dog, since your dog may spend the next several hours snoozing in a crate before your turn to compete.

Make sure your dog relieves itself before you enter the ring for warm-ups. If the unthinkable happens and your dog *does* foul the ring, tell a steward so that it can be cleaned up. An unchecked pool of urine on the entrance to the tunnel can ruin the scores of half the dogs entered in that day's competition. Likewise, if you see a dog foul the ring and the offender's handler does not report it, say something to the steward.

Your allotted time in the warm-up/familiarization session is usually five to ten minutes. When you get in the ring, do the following:

- Start with a couple of obstacles your dog is very familiar with to boost confidence.
- After that, concentrate on the unfamiliar obstacles.

165

- Make sure you do each of the obstacles in the ring at least once; your dog may have a problem with an obstacle that you don't anticipate.
- Check to see if the table or contact obstacles are slippery so you can be prepared to handle the obstacles accordingly. The obstacles should be set up in random order for the warm-up session, so you needn't bother trying to determine what the course arrangement will be for the first round.
- Don't feel obligated to work your dog for the entire time you are allotted. If your dog is comfortable on the course and tends to tire easily, save energy.
- In the rare event that you should encounter a safety hazard with any obstacle, bring it to the attention of the show committee or judge. If the problem is not corrected to your satisfaction, you have the right to ask that your entry fee(s) be refunded.

It usually takes thirty to sixty minutes to set up the first course after warm-ups. When the obstacles are in position, the number markers are set in place beside each obstacle and the judge measures the length of the course. Then you participate in a briefing by the judge.

JUDGE'S BRIEFING

In the judge's briefing, the judge informs you of the length of the course, the Standard Course Time (the time in which you must complete the course without incurring time faults), the Maximum Course Time (the maximum time you are allowed to run the course before the timekeeper blows a whistle and asks you to leave the ring), possible hazards and any unusual rules that may apply.

A few judging items at every event are left to the judge's discretion, and this briefing period is when these details are spelled out. This is particularly true in the Non-Standard classes, where many of the rules are left to the judge's discretion. If you have any questions about the rules or about how you will be scored, ask for clarification during the briefing.

WALKING THE COURSE

After the judge's briefing, you have the opportunity to become familiar with the course layout by walking the course. Since Agility trials are designed to test how your dog responds to your commands, your *dog* is *not allowed* to become familiar with the course before it is run (some dogs have excellent memories—even better than their handlers!).

Since you cannot take your dog with you when you walk the course, you must confine Star to a crate or arrange to have a spectator hold her for you.

One of the important things you can do to ensure your success is to treat the walking of the Agility course with the seriousness it deserves. Many novice exhibitors walk the course blindly, giving little or no thought to handling strategy. Besides memorizing the course, you should decide where you will position your dog and yourself at the start, how you are going to handle your dog to get the smoothest transitions from one obstacle to the next and how you are going to avoid traps.

Factors to consider when deciding how to handle your dog include level of training, experience and temperament. For example, if your dog is not trained to work off your right, don't try to do it in the ring. Or, if you have never left your dog at the start line in a competition, you may not want to try it for the first time at an important event. If the dog is easily stressed, any mistakes made in practice will probably be magnified in a show situation.

A small minority of dogs will perform better at a show than in practice. Only *you* can read your dog, and only you know how much of a gamble you are willing to take. The important thing is to decide, one way or another, how you will handle Star when you are in the ring before you both run the course.

Begin walking the course at the start line and decide how you will position your dog at the start. Remember:

- The farther behind the start line you position her, the faster she will be traveling when the timekeeper starts the clock.
- Choose a position that is most directly in line with the first obstacle.
- You can save time with a confident, quick dog if you leave her at the start, but if your dog is insecure at the start, it is usually better to run with her.
- Follow the numbers and decide on the best path for you and your dog.
- Decide when you will run with your dog on your left and when you will switch to your right.

Most courses include one or two traps, and it is imperative that you identify them when walking the course. There are different types of traps; two or more obstacles may be placed adjacent to one another, tempting the dog to take the wrong one, or there may be a sequence of obstacles that appear to the dog to have an obvious order but don't. Some traps may not be obvious to you. To determine what your dog will see, *get down at the dog's level and look at obstacles from the dog's point of view*.

Plan what you will do to prevent your dog from falling for each trap. Possible strategies may include positioning your body to block the dog's view of the incorrect obstacle, or timing a sharp control command such as "Come," "Heel," "Right" or "Left" while the dog is in midflight over the spread-bar jump. The strategies you choose to prevent your dog from succumbing to traps will often depend on whether you will be working ahead of, behind or alongside your dog. Your *start* strategy is simpler to determine in that you may position yourself anywhere in relation to the dog. Once you have begun running the course, however, your strategy will depend on the layout of the course, the

Walking the course with your "imaginary dog" before a competition.

speed of your dog and the amount of control you have at sending your dog ahead of you.

It's a good idea to walk the course as if you were actually handling your dog. You may feel a bit silly, but making the hand signals and performing the footwork will help you remember your plans when you are running the course "for real" and under stress. Walk the course as many times as possible in the time allotted or until you have the course and your strategy *completely memorized*. Even though the obstacles are numbered, you will not have time to look at the numbers when you run—you should be watching your dog and the upcoming obstacles.

PREPARING TO RUN

Before the competition starts, check with the steward to make sure you know what the running order will be (including jump-height order) and to find out if any exhibitors have failed to check in. Many an exhibitor has been caught off guard when a number is called early because of absentees.

Don't miss the opportunity to watch those going before you. What strategies have been working for most handlers and what haven't? What traps or problems have others experienced that you could avoid? Are dogs coming in substantially under standard course time? This observation will help you decide how fast you need to be. Also, the more dogs you watch, the better you will memorize the course.

Start waking up your dog at least five to ten minutes before you will be going into the ring—or sooner if your dog is a slow starter. Take her to relieve herself and insist that the dog make an attempt to appease you. This requires that you teach your dog to eliminate on command. You can do this by following your dog outside and giving your command along with praise *every time* Star eliminates. The command can be as subtle as "Let's do business" or "Hurry up." Your dog will soon learn what you want.

You would be wise to insist that your dog make at least a token attempt to urinate, because if your dog eliminates in the ring, you will be disqualified from the competition.

Get your dog limbered up by running, making sharp turns, throwing a ball or jumping over practice jumps, jumping sticks or short barriers. I've taught my dog to jump through my arms when I form a hoop with them. She enjoys the game, and I'm always carrying the "equipment" I need to warm up my dog.

Be ready to enter the ring when the steward instructs you to do so. Also make sure you are observing any restrictions on collars and leads before you enter. If the steward forgets to remind you to remove your dog's collar (at a sanctioned trial) and you run with it on your dog, you will be eliminated from the competition.

As you approach the start, take a look around the ring. After each dog's run, stewards are supposed to straighten weave poles, straighten the collapsed

A fun way to warm up your dog before entering the ring.
Photo: Gordon Simmons-Moake

tunnel and replace any displaced bars or boards on jumps. Stewards sometimes make mistakes. It's your responsibility to check these items before you run and inform the judge of anything that needs attention. If you don't, and, for example, the dog before you knocks down a bar, you may be penalized for displacing it, so check the course before you run!

RUNNING YOUR DOG

The timekeeper is usually the person who will tell you when you may start. The clock will start when the dog's nose crosses the start line. If the dog crosses the line before the timekeeper tells you he's ready, you will hear a whistle and the timekeeper will tell you to reposition your dog behind the line. If the dog crosses the line *after* the timekeeper tells you he's ready, the clock will start and you will not be allowed to restart, even if you were not ready.

Dogs love Agility, so be prepared to prevent your dog from starting without you. If you will be running alongside your dog from the start, you may hold on to your dog while waiting to begin; just remember not to touch her after you cross the start line. If you will be putting your dog in a stay behind the line while you position yourself on the course, don't take your eyes off the dog while you are doing so. Repeat the stay command if necessary. If the dog breaks

170

When "running your dog," do your best to follow the plan you have committed to memory—including controlling your dog on the contact zones.
Photo: Gene Abrahamson

Congratulating your teammate for a job well done.

position before you are ready, make the best of it and run the course—then vow to work on your stays under distracting conditions when you get home.

While running the course, do your best to follow the plan you have committed to memory. Your dog, being a dog, may have other ideas, in which case you will have to improvise. The most important thing is to keep at least one eye on your dog at all times. You can often see a dog "eyeing" an incorrect obstacle in time to prevent a mistake.

If your dog does make a mistake, take it in stride. We all have good days and bad days. Remember, you are an ambassador of our wonderful sport, so do your best to maintain its reputation of fun and good sportsmanship. Reprimanding your dog at the trial site is unthinkable, not to mention forbidden. Besides, most mistakes are the handler's fault!

No matter how you and your dog fare, you're a team, so remember to give your teammate a hug or handshake and some kind words as soon as you finish your run.

9

Holding an Agility Event

NOTHING fuels community interest in Agility as much as frequent local Agility events. Once you're bitten by the Agility bug, you may find that events within easy driving distance aren't as plentiful as you'd like. The answer—hold your own events. Even small training groups of five or six members can hold an event successfully, provided you can recruit the help of a few friends and family members. Your efforts will repay you with a showcase for your training efforts, while encouraging others to join in your sport.

FORMING A SHOW COMMITTEE

Every event needs a show committee to take charge of important details. Typically, responsibilities are as follows:

Trophy Chairperson: Orders ribbons, rosettes and trophies; ensures their arrival at the show site; solicits trophy donations prior to the event.

Hospitality Chairperson: Oversees the judge's travel arrangements; provides for the judge's comfort at the show site (meals, drinks, etc.).

Chief Ring Steward: Recruits and trains ring personnel; supervises stewards and equipment setup during course changes.

Trial Secretary: Prepares and mails all paperwork, including event flyers, judging schedules, catalogs and trial reports; accepts and logs entries; assigns armband numbers; supervises entries taken at the show site.

Equipment and Grounds Chairperson: Finds trial location; supervises equipment transportation, setup, teardown and site cleanup after the trial.

Trial Chairperson: Ensures committee members fulfill responsibilities; serves as "Field General" and handles problems at the show site.

CHOOSING THE TYPE OF EVENT

The first decision your show committee must make is what type of event to hold—a "sanctioned trial" or an informal "match." Sanctioned trials are held with the "blessing" of a national organization, such as the USDAA. Judging, obstacles and rules are standardized at a sanctioned trial, and your event-holding group must satisfy requirements set forth by the national organization. Informal matches are easier and less expensive to host than sanctioned trials since organizers are free to do as they please. You can decide to hold an event with very little advance notice and any knowledgeable person can judge. You don't need a complete set of obstacles, and your equipment need not conform to any standards. What's more, you may offer any competitive classes you desire, including those created by your imagination just for fun. Matches provide an excellent opportunity for new competitors to "get their feet wet," and give more experienced handlers the chance to try riskier handling techniques under show conditions.

CHOOSING A LOCATION

Perhaps the most difficult part about organizing an Agility event is finding a suitable location. A site with level terrain of grass or firmly packed dirt is the safest for the dogs since it provides a stable, low-impact jumping surface. You will need an area at least 80 feet by 100 feet reserved for the ring, with enough surrounding area to accommodate spectators and exhibitors.

Although it is easy to find inexpensive outdoor locations with adequate space, uncovered locations are risky. Rain, snow or intense heat can turn an otherwise pleasant event into an uncomfortable one for both dogs and exhibitors. You can minimize the discomfort by providing a covered area for crating dogs. Public parks with covered picnic or basketball shelters can often be reserved at no charge and are excellent places to attract spectators.

Another possible location is a covered livestock arena. Many arenas provide not only protection from the elements but spectator seating as well. When booking an arena, be sure to verify that the dirt floor will be hard-packed. Loose dirt provides poor footing for both dogs and handlers. Although you may be charged a fee to have the dirt rolled and packed before your event, the better footing is worth the cost. Unfortunately, most livestock arenas are neither heated nor air-conditioned.

Most indoor climate-controlled locations are unsuitable in that the flooring is smooth and hard and space is limited. Concrete is sometimes rough enough to provide the needed traction, but the impact is hard on the dogs' joints and paw pads. Although this may be acceptable for Obedience trials, where even advanced dogs are limited to three to seven jumps per day, it is *not* acceptable for Agility trials, where dogs may be asked to jump up to fifty times in one day. Another disadvantage of concrete is that falls can be much more dangerous than on any other surface. Consequently, if you hold an event on concrete, you *must* provide padded rubber matting. If you cannot cover the entire ring, at least cover the jumping areas. Partial matting complicates ring setup because you need to move the mats with each course change.

If the surface is smooth and slick, such as wood, linoleum or finished concrete, you *must* mat the entire ring. If you try to cover only selected portions of the ring, you will create a dangerous situation, since no two dogs or handlers take exactly the same path—especially in a class such as Gamblers where there is no set order to the obstacles.

If an indoor climate-controlled facility is a necessity and money is no object, there's another solution to consider. At the 1989 and 1990 USDAA national competitions at the Houston Astrodome, the problem of matting was handled in an elegant, though costly, manner. The show committee rented squares of sod to cover the entire 24,000-square-foot arena. Besides being attractive and providing good traction, the sod had a side benefit—if a dog fouled the ring, the soiled square could be quickly removed and replaced!

You can sometimes secure a desirable show site for free—complete with an abundance of spectators—by arranging to hold your trial in conjunction with another event such as a horse show, a state or county fair or a local festival. These events will often welcome an Agility trial as an added attraction—and what better opportunity to introduce the public to your favorite dog sport?

SECURING A JUDGE

For a sanctioned trial, you must have a licensed judge. You can obtain a list of licensed judges and a trial application form from the sanctioning national organization (see Appendix B). For a nonsanctioned event, anyone can judge.

For either a sanctioned or nonsanctioned event, send a letter of confirmation to the judge, thanking him or her for agreeing to participate and confirming any judging fees and/or travel reimbursements that will be made. Enclose a layout of the ring area that includes overall ring dimensions, type of surface and the locations of any trees, posts, sprinkler heads or other obstructions. Also include a list of all obstacles that will be available so that the judge can prepare course designs.

DECIDING WHAT CLASSES TO OFFER

People will travel great distances to earn Agility titles. To maximize the number of entries you receive, a USDAA-sanctioned event should include as many of the titling classes as possible. Consider projected entry figures for each class and time limitations to decide which classes to hold.

Whether you are holding a sanctioned or nonsanctioned event, classes such as Gamblers, Jumpers, Pairs Relay, Snooker and Open are fun for exhibitors and are always crowd pleasers. It's a good idea to include at least one of these classes if time permits.

Gamblers appeals to handlers at all levels, since those new to the sport can avoid obstacles with which they are experiencing problems, while advanced handlers can demonstrate distance control by attempting the "gamble." Gamblers is also appealing in that the course can be set quickly. If time limits you to only one Non-Standard class, Gamblers is an excellent choice.

Jumpers is a fast-moving and fun course to offer. The only constraint is that the host group must own or acquire a substantial number of hurdles—a minimum of eight and a maximum of twenty. If your group is short on hurdles, borrow Obedience competition "bar jumps" to help round out your set.

Pairs Relay is also fun. When offering Pairs, you must decide whether you will accept pairs with dogs of different jump heights. To do so may increase your Pairs entry, but will make it more difficult for the judge to design a challenging course since the hurdles cannot be used twice. Allowing pairs to have different jump height will also complicate and slow the running of the class.

Snooker requires handlers to demonstrate a large degree of control over their dogs. Without control, their dogs will fault and their runs will end abruptly. Therefore, if Snooker is new to your area, consider offering it as a two-round event. Allow each handler two attempts on the same course and add or average the scores to determine placements.

Open is a regular, numbered course similar to the titling classes—the difference being that you cannot earn titles from the Open class. The benefit of offering Open is that the host organization can establish the rules and restrictions for the class. For example, you can offer an Open class intended to attract newcomers that restricts titled dogs from entering, is judged at a slower speed or offers lower jump heights than Starters.

When determining how many and which classes to offer, consider your available time. The length of a trial is usually limited by the hours you have access to the show site, daylight or sheer stamina. Create a time budget of your proposed schedule to determine its feasibility. To do so, estimate the number of dogs you expect to enter and consider the following time factors:

- Unloading the equipment and setting it up will take about an hour. Registration can be held during setup to minimize delays.

176

- Equipment familiarization (warm-ups) takes about thirty minutes.
- It takes about forty-five minutes to arrange, measure and number a regular course. The course arrangements for Jumpers, Gamblers and Snooker classes can be set up in about thirty minutes.
- The briefing and walk-through together take about twenty minutes.
- Sometimes the judge will opt to use tighter obstacle spacing for dogs in the 12-inch and 18-inch height divisions and expand the spacing for dogs in the 24-inch and 30-inch divisions. In these cases, you must allow an extra twenty to forty minutes to move the obstacles, remeasure the course and allow exhibitors to walk the course with the new spacing.
- On a regular course twenty-five to thirty-five dogs can be judged in an hour, depending on the course, number of stewards and experience of the stewards and handlers. About thirty to forty dogs can be judged per hour in Gamblers, and fifty to seventy dogs in both Jumpers and Snooker.
- Allow ten to twenty-five minutes to tally scores and present awards, depending on the number of entries and the experience levels of the scorekeepers.

BUDGETING AND ENTRY FEES

An integral step in your trial-planning process is budgeting. To avoid losing money, your entry fees must cover all of your costs, so before you commit to a high-priced location or judge, make a list of all of your expenses. Aside from the location and judge's expenses (airfare, mileage, hotel, parking, meals, judging fee, judge's gift), add the costs of advertising, premium lists, catalogs, postage, prizes, refreshments, trailer (if necessary), PA system (if desired), armbands, etc. Subtract any estimated revenue from sources other than entry fees, such as concessions, donations and raffle tickets; then divide your remaining expenses by the number of people you think will enter. This is the amount you will need to collect from each exhibitor in the form of entry fees.

If your time budget allows you to offer several classes in one day, consider offering a "package fee" for the entire day's events. As a "package" incentive you can offer a special Grand Champion award to the dog with the best cumulative score from all classes—obviously, dogs must enter all classes on that day to be eligible to win! Offering Grand Champion awards in each jump-height division is an even greater incentive for competitors.

CHOOSING PRIZES

Your budget will help dictate what types of prizes you offer. Printed placement ribbons are the least expensive, followed by rosettes, then trophies. Trophies can take almost any form, from useful dog supplies to handmade items to traditional plaques or brass loving cups. A good rule of thumb is to provide placements to the top 20 to 30 percent of each class offered. Your expected entry estimate will determine how many placement prizes you should offer.

Because of the different challenges inherent to each size of dog, the most equitable competitions award placements only within jump-height categories, rather than having dogs of different height categories compete with one another. As a less-desirable compromise, some trials divide the four jump-height categories into two divisions—"Open Agility" (24 inches and 30 inches classes) and "Mini-Agility" (12 inches and 18 inches classes), awarding placements in each division.

DISTRIBUTING EVENT FLYERS

Almost all Agility events accept preentries (registration and payment) by mail. If you only accept entries at the door and the weather is miserable at your outdoor event, you may find yourself with few participants and a surplus of expenses. Preentries typically "close" (are no longer accepted) three to fourteen days before the event.

Whether the event will be sanctioned or nonsanctioned, you need to provide a flyer that contains all pertinent information, including the following:

- Date, time and location of the event
- Whether held indoors or outdoors, covered or uncovered, and type of jumping surface (if not obvious)
- Description of classes and entry limits, if any
- What rules will be used
- List of obstacles that will be used
- Whether it is a sanctioned event (and if so, by what organization)
- One (or more) contact person's name, address and phone number
- Judge's name(s)
- Entry form asking for dog's name, breed and jump height; handler's name, address and phone number; classes entered; waiver of liability with a space for a required signature (The waiver helps protect the sponsoring group from liability for any injury that may occur at the show site. The USDAA can provide you with a sample waiver to include in your flyers for USDAA-sanctioned events.)
- Description of prizes to be awarded
- Closing date for entries, if any
- Entry fees and method of payment
- Announcements about crating, show site rules, refund policy, etc.
- List of nearby hotels that will accept dogs

178

PROCESSING ENTRIES

Once entries close, the show secretary assigns armband numbers to participants. You can acquire armbands from pet food manufacturers either with or without preprinted numbers. When assigning armband numbers, leave some unassigned numbers for those who enter at the show if you will be accepting entries at the door.

If you accept preentries by mail, you should send exhibitors a written notice confirming their entries. The notice should provide the starting time for registration and warm-ups so that exhibitors know when to arrive and directions to the show site. It's best not to list starting times for each class, since the amount of time it takes to arrange equipment varies greatly depending on the courses the judge designs.

A catalog of exhibitors is always appreciated by spectators and exhibitors alike. The catalog should provide a list of the dogs in each class, including the armband number, handler's name and address and dog's name and breed. The breed is useful for helping spectators follow the catalog and the dogs running when it is difficult to read the armband numbers.

BEFORE THE SHOW

A day or two before your Agility event takes place, call the judge to confirm travel arrangements. Arrange for the judge to arrive at the show site at least fifteen minutes before warm-ups begin so that any measurement disputes can be resolved and participants can warm up at the appropriate jump height.

Make final assignments by determining who will be the following:

- Registration stewards (2 or 3)—can double as scorekeepers when registration is over
- Course setup crew, also called "course builders" (5 or more)
- Timekeeper (someone who is very responsible and alert!)
- Scorekeepers (2)
- Announcer
- Ring stewards (2) and gate steward (1)—can double as course builders
- Scribe, if desired by the judge
- Runner—can double as course builder

To prepare for the big day, make a checklist of things to take with you to the show site. When putting on our first Agility match, we forgot to take along several things, the most critical of which was a pooper scooper!

It's easiest to set up the equipment the night before but it's not always possible. If not, you will need to arrive at the site at the earliest possible time so that judging gets underway at a reasonable hour.

On the way to the show site, place dog show signs at strategic intersections to help exhibitors find their way. You can obtain dog show signs for little or no cost from some pet food manufacturers.

RESPONSIBILITIES AT THE TRIAL

At the event site, show personnel assume their prearranged responsibilities to ensure that all goes smoothly during the day's activities. In addition to the show committee members, other on-site personnel include:

Course Builders

Upon arrival, the **course builders** should begin placing the equipment randomly around the course with a minimum distance of 15 feet between obstacles. If the judge is on-site during your initial setup, ask for an approximate location of the heavy pieces such as the dog walk, A-frame and cross-over. After warm-ups, the judge provides a written layout of the first course and the course builders arrange the equipment per the judge's design. This is called "roughing out" the course. Afterward, the judge "fine-tunes" the positioning of each obstacle.

Stewards

While the equipment is being set up for warm-ups, the **registration stewards** can set up and begin distributing armbands. Since check-in involves measuring the dogs to ensure that they are entered in the correct jump-height divisions, having three stewards at the table is preferable—two to check people in and hand out armbands and one to measure dogs. Because the measurement of the dog's height is critical, most host organizations use "wickets" to determine the dogs' jump heights. Wickets are usually U-shaped devices of a fixed dimension that determine whether a dog is above or below a certain height. It's important to have a level surface for measuring, so if smooth flooring will not be available, bring along a board to use as a level surface, or use the pause table. If a dog's measurement appears to be borderline between two jump-height divisions, ask the judge to measure the dog and give a ruling.

During warm-ups, the **gate steward** calls dogs in small groups of similar jump heights and times a five- or ten-minute warm-up period. During competition, this steward calls exhibitors to the ring gate and ensures that exhibitors remove their dogs' collars. To keep the trial moving smoothly, the gate steward should have the next exhibitor ready to enter the ring as each performing exhibitor crosses the finish line.

During the competition, between runs, you will need two **ring stewards** to straighten the collapsed tunnel chute and weave poles (if necessary), and to replace any hurdle bars or boards that may have been displaced by the previous dog. The ring stewards also change jump heights between classes.

180

In addition to gate and ring stewards, you will also need a **runner** to run scores from the judge (or scribe) to the scoring table.

Timekeeper

Before the competition, the judge briefs the **timekeeper** about the timing of the first class. The timekeeper begins each dog's run in a position in line with the "Start" markers and ends directly in line with the "Finish" markers.

Scorekeepers and Scribe

Because of the importance of accurate scorekeeping, it's best to have two **scorekeepers** so they can check each other's work. While exhibitors are walking the course, the scorekeepers can enter the dogs' names, armband numbers and the Standard Course Time on the scorepads and composite score sheets. The scorepads contain "Agility judging sheets," one of which is used for each dog's run.

Some judges prefer to signal faults to a **scribe** rather than mark the judging sheets themselves. While dogs are running, the scribe watches only the judge at all times, avoiding the temptation to watch the performances of the dogs in the ring. As the judge signals faults, the scribe makes notations on the Agility judging sheets. For Standard classes and others that use a Standard Course Time,

Agility judging sheets.

Single-Round Agility Competition Score Sheet

Competition: _FlashPaws 11/24/91_ Class: _Starters – 12" dogs_ SCT: _80_

	Team No.	Dog No.	Dog's Time	Time Faults	Course Faults (or Points)	Total Faults (or Points)	Place
1.		100	73.87	0	0	0	Q
2.		101	82.21	2.21	10	12.21	
3.		102	70.18	0	0	0	2Q
4.		103	76.54	0	15	15	
5.		104	79.93	0	5	5	
6.		105	86.44	6.44	0	6.44	
7.		106	E	—	—	E	
8.		107	81.97	1.97	5	6.97	
9.		108	80.37	.37	0	.37	
10.		109	72.46	0	0	0	3Q
11.		110	78.93	0	5	5	
12.		✗	abs	—	—	abs	
13.		112	92.26	12.26	5	17.26	
14.		113	82.03	2.03	0	2.03	
15.		114	68.81	0	5	5	
16.		115	72.22	0	10	10.00	
17.		116	79.13	0	0	0	Q
18.		117	89.06	9.06	10	19.06	
19.		118	69.11	0	0	0	1Q
20.		119	73.68	0	0	0	4Q
21.							
22.							
23.							
24.							
25.							
26.							

182

Two-Round Agility Competition Score Sheet

Competition: FlashPaws Regional   **Class:** 30" dogs

Round 1 SCT: 75
Round 2 SCT: 65

	Team No.	Dog No.	Round 1 Total Faults / Points / Dog's Time	Round 2 Total Faults / Points / Dog's Time	Total Faults	Total Time	Place
1.		401	0 / 63.33	6.29 / 71.29	6.29	134.62	
2.		402	0 / 68.28	0 / 54.99	0	123.27	4
3.		403	7.66 / 77.66	1.21 / 66.21	8.87	143.87	
4.		404	0 / 74.43	0 / 63.06	0	137.49	
5.		405	5 / 73.26	5 / 61.08	10	134.34	
6.		406	0 / 62.37	0 / 59.91	0	122.28	3
7.		407	5 / 64.46	0 / 58.03	5	122.49	
8.		408	0 / 73.19	5.28 / 70.28	5.28	143.47	
9.		409	0 / 70.45	.06 / 65.06	.06	135.51	
10.		410	26.02 / 91.02	15.68 / 70.68	41.70	161.70	
11.		411	9.65 / 84.65	5.51 / 65.51	15.16	150.16	
12.		412	0 / 59.90	0 / 54.36	0	114.26	1
13.		413	0 / 61.19	0 / 53.32	0	114.51	2
14.		414	1.65 / 76.65	0 / 59.87	1.65	136.52	
15.							
16.							
17.							
18.							

REGULAR Total Faults/Time • GAMBLERS Total Points/Time • SNOOKER Total Points/Time   © 1990 FlashPaws

the scribe uses a Standard judging sheet. Course faults are assessed in increments of five (minor faults) or twenty (failure to perform an obstacle). These are marked as they occur on the large white area of the judging sheet. Although Standard judging sheets can be used for all classes, when judging Gamblers or Snooker, it helps to have a specialized type of judging sheet. Instead of marking faults, the scribe marks points accumulated.

The scorekeepers double-check the scribe's tabulations for each dog's judging sheet and then transfer the information to a composite score sheet containing all the dogs' scores. For two-round events, such as tournaments, it is more efficient to use a composite score sheet specifically designed for these events. The scorekeepers use the information on the score sheet to determine the award placements, which are usually double-checked by the judge. Because many groups use a separate score sheet for each height division in each class, it helps to have a "cover sheet" to summarize the classes held and to identify the Agility event to which the score sheets belong.

Exhibitors are always appreciative when scores are posted after each dog runs. If you have enough manpower, an additional steward can copy the scores from the composite score sheets onto the posted scoreboard as each dog's score is recorded.

Announcer

Having an **announcer** and a portable PA system lends an air of excitement to the event. A knowledgeable announcer can help educate the audience while providing the names and scores of exhibitors.

IN CONCLUSION

Despite all your careful plans and hard work, things often can and will go wrong. By taking preventive measures and making contingency plans, you can avoid certain disasters. For example:

- Be prepared for the likely event that some of your helpers will cancel or not show up. Schedule more than the bare minimum number of stewards you will need.
- If you are flying in a judge from another city, try not to book him or her on the latest possible flight. With airline delays and cancellations always a possibility, the judge may not make it to your event on time.
- Prepare for the possibility that your equipment may become damaged during loading/unloading or in transit by bringing along a set of tools and spare hardware.

Your experiences will help make each trial you hold better than your last. At our first sanctioned Agility trial (which was held outdoors at a public park),

Agility Trial

Competition: FlashPaws Agility Training Center

U S D A A - Sanctioned Event

Date: November 24, 1991

Location: Montgomery County Fairgrounds

New Caney, Texas

Judge: I. C. Faults

Class	Course Length (Yds.)	SCT (Seconds)
Starters	160	80
Novice	160	80
Advanced	190	75
Masters	180	60
Gamblers	50 secs. / gamble 15 secs.	N / A
Jumpers	175	45

Agility trial cover sheet.

© 1990 FlashPaws

we had torrential rains, hail, thunder and lightning. On top of all this, it was cold and damp in the morning and steamy hot in the afternoon. As if this weren't enough, our pipe tunnel blew out of the trailer somewhere en route to the show site—never to be found again. Ever since then, all of our events have been held in a covered location. The diminished stress factor alone makes it worth the cost! We also rent an enclosed truck instead of an open trailer. The equipment stays safe and dry and it always makes it to the show.

10

Just for the Fun of It— Create Your Own Activities and Obstacles

---

Not EVERYONE has the time or the inclination to work toward competitive levels of Agility. Whatever your reasons, a purely recreational approach to Agility can be a fun and rewarding way to spend some spare time with one of your best friends, your dog.

IDEAS FOR OBSTACLES—ASSEMBLY VS. CONSTRUCTION

When competition is not your goal, your Agility obstacles can be of any design imaginable. By all means, make them easier to master—there is no need to make them as challenging as competition obstacles unless you want to.

To create inexpensive Agility obstacles quickly and without investing hours of labor, think in terms of "assembled" rather than "constructed" obstacles. You should be able to find most of the ingredients for your obstacles around your home. If not, you can probably purchase them easily and inexpensively. Here are a few ideas:

Tunnels

Create a maze of tunnels by taping together large cardboard appliance boxes. The maze won't last forever, but while it's assembled, it will bring your dogs hours of pleasure. For a more permanent tunnel, you can purchase a child's play tunnel at a toy store. These often fold flat in a box that you can easily store under a bed or in a closet.

To make a collapsed tunnel, start with a plastic garbage pail with the bottom cut out. Then tie a sheet or tarp around the rim of the pail using a luggage strap or cord. When using your collapsed tunnel, you will need to hold it steady between two supports to keep it from rolling or moving. For a more permanent solution, attach the pail to a plywood base.

Tire/Hoop Jumps

Suspend a plastic Hula-Hoop between two chairs or attached to two plungers (plumber's helpers) using duct tape. Hula-Hoops are much easier for the dog to jump through than tires since the openings are so much larger. They are also lighter, less expensive and easier to store than tires.

If you prefer to use a tire, you can rest it on the ground while supporting it on each side by chairs or other sturdy supports. To elevate it off the ground requires a more elaborate setup. If you do use a tire, be sure to wrap tape around

Having fun with backyard Agility.

it to prevent the dogs from catching their feet on the "lip" while they are jumping through it.

Weave Poles

You can assemble inexpensive weave poles using lengths of PVC plastic pipe driven into the ground. (Procedures are provided in Appendix A.) For weave poles that are even easier to set up, tear down and adjust, use traffic cones or plungers. Although competition weave poles are spaced about 20 inches apart, there is no reason yours can't be spaced much wider and staggered to encourage early success. When you first begin, you can position the poles wide enough apart so that you can weave through them with your dog.

Hurdles

You can assemble hurdles out of almost any objects found around your home. Try suspending poles such as broomsticks, closet poles or lengths of PVC pipe from any objects that will support them. Lawn chairs, crates, boxes, cans and buckets are just a few ideas to get you started. For variety, you can make solid-looking hurdles by draping sheets or towels over suspended poles. For safety, construct your hurdles so that the pole or board can be easily knocked off if the dog hits it.

For a long jump, try using scalloped concrete lawn edging. The larger your dog, the more edging you will need. Rest poles (PVC, closet poles, etc.) in the "valleys" between the scallops to create a row of poles for your dog to jump.

Pause Obstacles

For a pause table, connect several sturdy, plastic "milk-crate-style" organizer bins by wrapping duct tape or nylon cord through the plastic mesh sides. You will need enough crates so that when they are turned upside down, they form a platform measuring about 3 feet square by 1 foot high. Then, attach a sheet of Masonite (rough side up) to the plastic mesh on the top of the platform.

The pause box is easy to make. As an added bonus, it stores easily and can be disassembled in seconds for even more convenient storage. You will find procedures for making a pause box in Appendix A.

Contact Obstacles

Make a plank for the dogs to walk across by resting a sturdy board on two storage crates or on cement blocks. A $2'' \times 12'' \times 8'$ board will provide enough of a challenge without being too difficult for the dog to master.

To include other contact obstacles such as the see-saw, A-frame or dog walk in your just-for-fun Agility setup, you will probably need to do some actual building. The inclined ramps require that your equipment be sturdy, and nothing found around the home can safely fill your needs. To build contact obstacles, use the construction plans in the Appendix A and modify them to make your obstacles lower, smaller, wider, etc., to accommodate your dogs.

Whatever obstacles you build or assemble, make sure that they are absolutely safe for your dogs.

IDEAS FOR ACTIVITIES

Use your imagination. Enjoyable activities could include one-on-one play/ practice for "quality time" with your dog, an Agility party for your dog and a few of its closest "friends" or a public exhibition. Whatever the activity, do it only on a low-impact surface with good traction such as grass or packed dirt— not on concrete!

One-on-One Agility

One of the best places to have fun with Agility is in your own backyard. To introduce your dog to his new backyard "amusement park," convey to Phideaux at the start that it is intended for his recreation and enjoyment. You can do this by incorporating some of your usual games into Agility practice on the obstacle course. Here are some examples:

- Throw a ball or stick over a low hurdle to encourage the dog to jump over it. Then encourage a return to you by jumping the hurdle with the retrieved object in his mouth.
- Play "follow-the-leader" or "chase me" by running from your dog while you jump over low hurdles yourself, encouraging him to follow in your path. Then turn around and chase him.
- Call the dog through the Hula-Hoop/tire and tunnels, perhaps enlisting the help of a friend. As soon as the dog lands after jumping (or exits the tunnel), throw a ball for him to retrieve.

After your dog has decided he loves the new playground, introduce Phideaux to the new games of zig-zagging through the weave poles, walking the plank and jumping on the pause table. He should be very receptive and eager to participate. To maintain enthusiasm, integrate periods of horseplay in between trying new obstacles.

Even though your Agility practice is just for fun, choose and use commands for each obstacle as described in chapter 3, Obstacle Training. This will give you a common language for referring to obstacles when playing on your Agility equipment.

An Agility Party

Once you've invested some time and creativity in assembling your backyard Agility course, you can share the fun with your friends and their dogs by holding an Agility party. This can be as informal as calling your friends over on a whim and letting them "have a go"; or you can go all-out with invitations, planned activities, prizes—even doggy refreshments! You may think this is more fun for the owners than the dogs, but when you see how much the dogs enjoy themselves, you'll know otherwise. Whatever you do, don't forget to have a loaded camera or camcorder nearby to record the day's fun.

At your Agility party you can allow your guests to play on their own or organize some games for which you can award prizes. Probably the best idea is to include a bit of both. Although the possibilities are endless, here are a few ideas for organized games:

- Set up four low hurdles in a straight line, 15 feet apart, and see who can call his or her dog over the greatest number of hurdles without the dog going around them. Start with each owner calling his or her dog over one hurdle. Multiple commands, tapping the jump, cheering, etc., are all permissible. Then add a second, then a third, then a fourth. In the unlikely event that everyone at your party is a "ringer" and has no difficulty calling their dogs over four hurdles, toughen the rules by requiring each dog to hold a ball or toy in its mouth while jumping.
- Have someone hold each dog at the opening of the pipe tunnel while the owners go to the other side. Use a stopwatch to see who can call his or her dog through the fastest.
- See who can get his or her dog to jump on the pause table from the farthest distance away. If none of the dogs do well at this, allow each dog a practice round with the owners placing treats on the far side of the table. Then try again without the treats.
- Do the obvious and set up a numbered course that owners and their dogs must follow. You can make number markers out of inverted disposable drinking cups.

Public Agility

You can occasionally set up your equipment in a public place to share your new recreational outlet with an even larger group of people. An appropriate location for a fun-type Agility obstacle course is at the scene of a fund-raising event such as a local humane society benefit. You can provide demonstrations and perhaps even allow the public to try the course with their dogs. In this way you can offer an enjoyable outing for local dogs and their owners while helping to attract support for a worthy cause.

Whenever your equipment will be used by the public, be doubly sure that it is safe and sturdy for dogs of all sizes. You may also want to ask participants to sign a waiver of liability to protect you in case of any accident. Check with the nonprofit organization hosting the event for advice in this matter.

IN CONCLUSION

Recreational Agility demands very little of your time and your money—you can participate whenever your schedule allows. It's perfect for people who just love their dogs and want to spend more time with them but have no interest in competition. The next time your dog puts his head on your lap and his eyes say, "Let's do something!," you will have a few more ideas for fun and recreation.

EPILOGUE AND APPENDICES

---

dog's eyes watching you longingly from the window as you work with younger siblings is almost too much to bear. A Veterans class could keep both dogs and handlers enjoying the sport longer—and isn't that what Agility should be about?

APPENDIX A

Obstacle Construction

by Gordon Simmons-Moake

THIS APPENDIX will show you how to build the Agility equipment necessary to train and to hold competitions. The equipment is designed to be sturdy and easy to assemble and disassemble. Most of the designs have been tested extensively in our classes, and the others reflect recent modifications that were made to solve problems, improve safety, simplify use or facilitate construction. In the interest of brevity, I will assume that you are familiar with wood construction techniques and tools.

The plans listed in this appendix meet all USDAA specifications at the time of this writing. Nevertheless, if USDAA compatibility is your goal, it is recommended that you check the current obstacle requirements at any time before you begin construction. (Construction standards are listed in the *Official Rules and Regulations of the United States Dog Agility Association.*) You could also benefit from examining the Agility equipment of other groups.

It is also recommended that you use weather-resistant materials, build all equipment out of treated lumber and try to use plastic wherever possible. Multiple coats of paint are also helpful in protecting your investment.

These obstacle plans are based on proven designs and are intended to provide rugged, safe equipment. However, the quality and safety of the obstacles will depend on the materials you use and your construction techniques. It is up to *you* to verify that the equipment is adequate for your needs.

Construction is much easier if you have a full arsenal of power tools at your disposal. Although they are not all necessary, your work will be easier if you have a radial arm saw, circular saw, band saw, table saw, drill, drill press, saber saw, belt sander and electric screwdriver. Common hand tools are also required. Once the parts are cut, assembly takes a long time because of the many screws that are usually required. You will save a lot of time if you have a pilot drill bit for #8 screws. (This simultaneously drills the three different hole diameters for a wood screw.) During the assembly stage, the electric screwdriver becomes your most valuable tool; I stop work when the batteries run low. Try to buy screws with Phillips heads, since they are easier to drive than those with slotted heads.

It is important that your equipment be free from splinters and sharp edges, so be sure to sand the obstacles before painting. This is often easiest to do before the component pieces are assembled.

Because of similarities in construction techniques and materials, all of the contact obstacles are in one section and the hurdles in another. The first section, labeled Essential Miscellaneous, consists of everything else. You may find it useful to refer to the illustrations of completed obstacles in chapters 1 and 3.

Essential Miscellaneous

Weave Poles

Materials for two sets of five poles (one complete set):

2 ea.	1" × 4" × 8'
2 ea.	¼" Masonite, 12" × 8'
10 ea.	¾" PVC × 39"
10 ea.	¾" threaded PVC caps
10 ea.	threaded male coupler
10 ea.	¾" unthreaded PVC caps
10 ea.	#10-32 × 1-½" flat-head machine screws
10 ea.	²¹⁄₃₂" (or close) rubber faucet washers
20 ea.	#10-32 nuts
10 ea.	#10 or ³⁄₁₆" washers
24 ea.	¼" washers
4 ea.	¼" × 1-½" carriage bolts
4 ea.	¼" nuts

Weave poles consist of five to twelve poles that are 3 to 4 feet high and are spaced at equal intervals of 18" to 24". They can be either rigidly or semirigidly mounted. I much prefer semirigidly mounted poles since they allow the dogs to weave faster and thereby provide greater spectator appeal.

You can create a simple set of weave poles by driving ¾" PVC pipe into the ground with a hammer. If your ground is too hard for this, you can use galvanized steel pipe, either as the poles themselves or to make holes in which to place PVC poles. A compromise between the two is to drive stakes into the

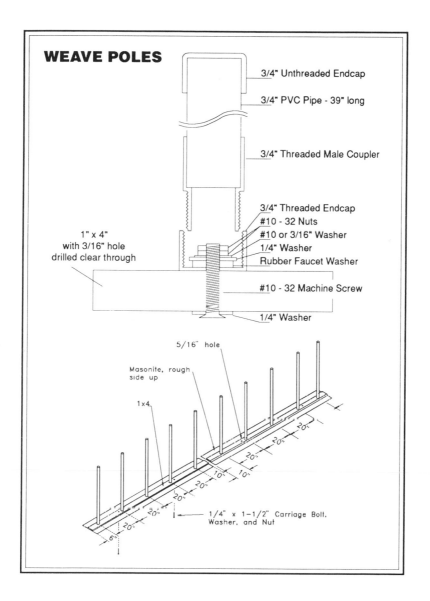

WEAVE POLES

3/4" Unthreaded Endcap

3/4" PVC Pipe - 39" long

3/4" Threaded Male Coupler

3/4" Threaded Endcap
#10 - 32 Nuts
#10 or 3/16" Washer
1/4" Washer
Rubber Faucet Washer

1" x 4"
with 3/16" hole
drilled clear through

#10 - 32 Machine Screw

1/4" Washer

5/16" hole

Masonite, rough
side up

1x4

20"
20"
20"
10"
10"
20"
20"
20"
20"
6"

1/4" x 1-1/2" Carriage Bolt,
Washer, and Nut

ground and place PVC pipe over them. You can also drill holes in a 1" × 10" wooden board to hold the poles.

Most competition poles are mounted on 1" × 4"s. For indoor use the 1" × 4"s are mounted on Masonite, which provides stability without hindering the dogs' movement. Outdoors the 1" × 4"s are sometimes staked to the ground, but it is strongly recommended that you keep them mounted on the Masonite, since 1" × 4"s without the Masonite tend to fall over unless they are staked. Surprisingly, the Masonite can withstand years of weathering without deteriorating. Some people attach rubber furniture feet or the rubber tips of crutches to the 1″ × 4″ to hold the poles. The stretch of the rubber allows the poles to give, providing a desirable, semirigid mounting. Unfortunately, repeated stretching causes the rubber to weaken and rip; the poles are then too loose and tend to fall out.

Others have solved the problem by rigidly mounting galvanized pipes to the 1″ × 4″ by screwing them into threaded steel flanges. PVC is sometimes slipped over the pipes for appearance. Although this provides truly rugged poles, they are very heavy and result in less spectacular weaves by the dogs. Although PVC poles can be screwed into the flanges instead of steel pipe, sudden impacts on the PVC poles tend to snap them at the flange. This design uses PVC poles attached with inexpensive PVC fixtures in a semirigid manner. Flexibility of the pole comes from compressing a rubber faucet washer. PVC poles and mountings can be used since the flexibility will allow the poles to bend without breaking at the base.

As is common in the United States, this design consists of two 8-foot sections of five weave poles each. The poles are positioned at 20-inch intervals, but the distance from the end to the first pole is different for the two ends. Thus, when the two sections are put together to form ten poles, the sections must be properly oriented to obtain 20-inch spacing between the fifth and sixth poles.

To construct the weave poles:

- Drill a ³⁄₁₆-inch hole in the threaded end caps and in the 1″ × 4″ where the end caps go.
- Then attach the end caps to the 1″ × 4″ as shown. Use two nuts with the mounting bolt so that vibration will not loosen the end cap.
- Next, attach the Masonite (rough side up). Use PVC cement to attach the threaded couplers and unthreaded end caps to the PVC poles. You can improve the appearance of your poles by removing the ink printed on the PVC. (Acetone works well, but it is nasty and should be used with care.)

Before screwing the poles into the end caps, make sure the threads on the poles are free of dirt, and apply a light coat of grease or petroleum jelly to the threads. Screw the poles in moderately tight; hand tightening should be sufficient. Make sure the poles are screwed in more than one or two turns or they may break. So far the only poles that we've had break were not screwed in properly. Since a pole could possibly break whenever you assemble your equipment, it always pays to have a few extra poles and threaded end caps, particularly at a competition.

Occasionally, the threaded end caps may become loose. When this happens, remove the poles and Masonite, and tighten the nuts on the mounting bolts.

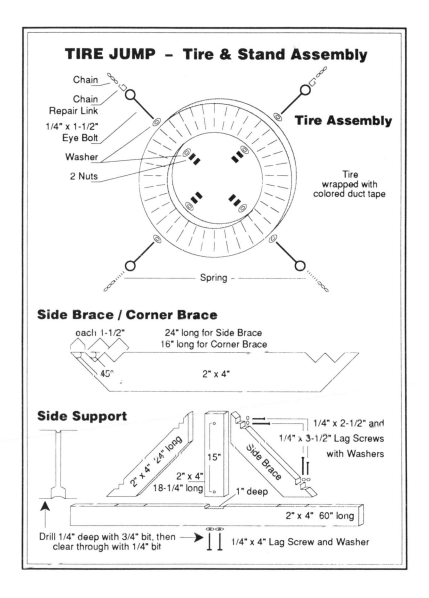

TIRE JUMP – Tire & Stand Assembly

Tire Assembly

Chain
Chain
Repair Link
1/4" x 1-1/2"
Eye Bolt
Washer
2 Nuts

Tire
wrapped with
colored duct tape

Spring

Side Brace / Corner Brace

each 1-1/2"

24" long for Side Brace
16" long for Corner Brace

45°

2" x 4"

Side Support

2" x 4" 24" long

15"

Side Brace

2" x 4"
18-1/4" long

1" deep

1/4" x 2-1/2" and
1/4" x 3-1/2" Lag Screws
with Washers

2" x 4" 60" long

Drill 1/4" deep with 3/4" bit, then →
clear through with 1/4" bit

1/4" x 4" Lag Screw and Washer

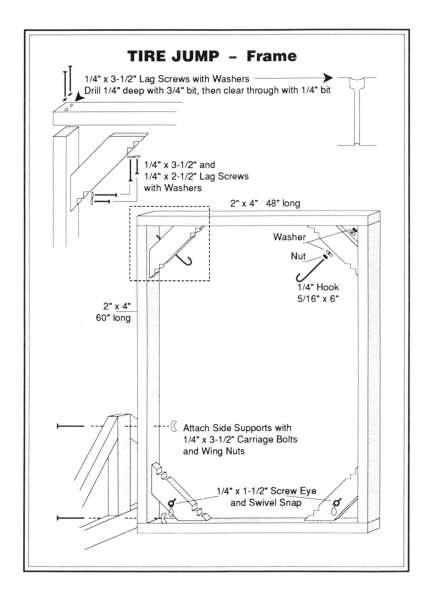

TIRE JUMP – Frame

1/4" x 3-1/2" Lag Screws with Washers
Drill 1/4" deep with 3/4" bit, then clear through with 1/4" bit

1/4" x 3-1/2" and
1/4" x 2-1/2" Lag Screws
with Washers

2" x 4"   48" long

Washer

Nut

1/4" Hook
5/16" x 6"

2" x 4"
60" long

Attach Side Supports with
1/4" x 3-1/2" Carriage Bolts
and Wing Nuts

1/4" x 1-1/2" Screw Eye
and Swivel Snap

Tire Jump

Materials:

4 ea.	2″ × 4″ × 60″ (frame and side support)		2 ea.	5/16″ × 6″ clothesline hooks
2 ea.	2″ × 4″ × 48″ (frame)		4 ea.	5/16″ flat washers
2 ea.	2″ × 4″ × 18-1/4″ (side support)		2 ea.	5/16″ nuts
4 ea.	2″ × 4″ × 16″, cut as shown (corner brace)		2 ea.	1/4″ × 1-1/2″ screw eyes
4 ea.	2″ × 4″ × 24″, cut as shown (side braces)		4 ea.	1/4″ × 1″ eye bolts
16 ea.	1/4″ × 2-1/2″ lag screws		8 ea.	1/4″ nuts
24 ea.	1/4″ × 3-1/2″ lag screws		8 ft.	2/0 tenso chain
4 ea.	1/4″ × 4″ lag screws		4 ea.	chain repair links
52 ea.	1/4″ flat washers		2 ea.	swivel snaps
4 ea.	3-1/2″ carriage bolts		2 ea.	springs (about 1/16″-thick wire, 4″ long)
4 ea.	1/4″ wing nuts		1 ea.	tire, 15″ to 20″ inner diameter, 28″ or greater outer diameter

The tire jump consists of a tire, a frame from which the tire is hung and two side supports that keep the frame upright. First, build two side supports. Notice that the side braces are notched to facilitate screwing them to the rest of the side support. Instead of cutting the notches, you can drill and counterbore the holes, but this is much more difficult. Next, build the frame and attach the side supports. Then attach the hooks and eyes to the frame.

The outer diameter of the tire must be at least 28 inches, and the inner diameter must be between 15 inches and 20 inches. Bolt the eye hooks in place very tightly and wrap the tire in duct tape. Wrap several layers on the bottom since dogs will be pushing off from the inside of the tire. Use colored duct tape on the last layer to add style. Then drill about three 1/4-inch holes in the bottom of the tire to allow any water that seeps in to drain out.

Pause Table

Materials for 12″ table:

4 ea.	1″ × 2″ × 35-1/4″ (frame)		1 ea.	piece of outdoor carpeting, 42″ × 42″
1 ea.	1″ × 2″ × 34-1/2″ (frame)		8 ea.	#8 × 2″ wood screws
4 ea.	1″ × 4″ × 11-1/2″ (legs)		8 ea.	1/4″ × 2″ carriage bolts
1 ea.	1/2″ plywood, 36″ × 36″ (top)		8 ea.	1/4″ wing nuts (or washer and regular nut)
			1 box	1-1/4″ ringed nails
			1 box	9/16″ staples

PAUSE TABLES

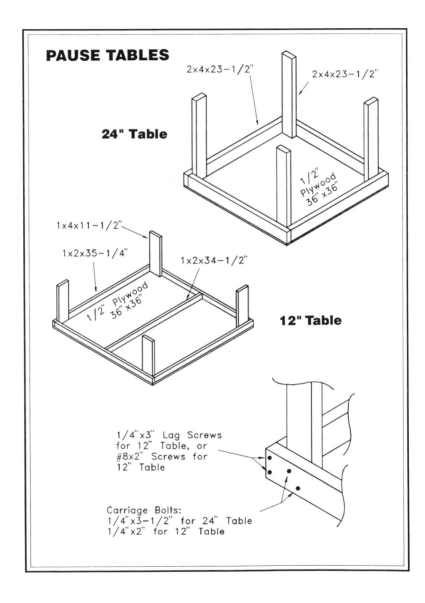

2x4x23-1/2"

2x4x23-1/2"

24" Table

1/2" Plywood 36"x36"

1x4x11-1/2"

1x2x35-1/4"

1x2x34-1/2"

1/2" Plywood 36"x36"

12" Table

1/4"x3" Lag Screws for 12" Table, or #8x2" Screws for 12" Table

Carriage Bolts:
1/4"x3-1/2" for 24" Table
1/4"x2" for 12" Table

204

Materials for 24" table:

4 ea.	2" × 4" × 34-½" (frame)	8 ea.	¼" × 3" lag screws
4 ea.	2" × 4" × 23-½" (legs)	8 ea.	¼" washers (for use with lag screws)
1 ea.	½" plywood, 36" × 36" (top)	8 ea.	¼" × 3-½" carriage bolts
1 ea.	piece of outdoor carpeting, 46" × 46"	8 ea.	¼" wing nuts (or washer and regular nut)
		1 box	1-¼" ringed nails
		1 box	⁹⁄₁₆" staples

Although a different height table can be used for each jump-height category, only two are commonly used—one 12 inches high for the 12 inch and 18-inch jump heights, and one 24 inches high for the 24-inch and 30-inch jump heights. Although the 12-inch table could be the same style as the 24-inch table, the 12-inch design is lighter.

Construction is similar for both tables. Assemble the frame. Then,

- Drill ⁵⁄₁₆-inch holes in one of the legs, making sure to drill them straight. Then use this leg as a template to mark hole positions in each corner of the frame.
- On the frame, mark each board so that the frame can be reassembled in the same manner, and then disassemble it.
- Drill straight ⁵⁄₁₆-inch holes in the frame pieces where you marked them, and reassemble the frame.
- Now nail the plywood onto the top of the frame.
- Place the other three legs in position at a corner and drill holes through the holes in the frame into the legs. All four legs should now be interchangeable.
- With the legs off, cover the table with outdoor carpeting, stapling it to the bottom of the frame.
- Then cut holes in the fabric where your bolt holes are.
- Finally, bolt the legs in place using either wing nuts or a washer and nuts. (Wing nuts make disassembly easy, but regular nuts can be made tighter.)

Pause Box

Materials:

4 ea.	¾" PVC pipe × 48"
4 ea.	¾" PVC elbows
4 ea.	¾" 16D nails (optional)

The pause box is easy to make. Just cut four pieces of PVC pipe and push them into four PVC elbows. To keep the box in place, drill a ³⁄₁₆-inch hole 2 inches from one end of each bar, through which you can hammer a 16D nail.

Collapsed Tunnel

Materials:

1 ea.	chute		2 ea.	4" × (barrel length)
1 ea.	strap			adhesive, nonslip tape
1 ea.	barrel (18" to 20" inner		4 ea.	¼" × 2" lag screws
	diameter, 30" or less in		4 ea.	¼" × 3" lag screws
	length)		2 ea.	¼" × 1-½" carriage
1 ea.	¾" plywood (4" shorter			bolts
	than barrel) × 42"		10 ea.	¼" flat washers
2 ea.	2" × 4" × (barrel		2 ea.	¼" nuts
	outer diameter + ¼")		16 ea.	#8 × 1-¼" wood
1 ea.	2" × 4" × (barrel			screws
	outer diameter + 3")			
8 ea.	1" × 2" × 2" (feet)			

The collapsed tunnel consists of a short rigid opening with a 12-foot-long tubular piece of fabric (called a chute) attached to the exit. This fabric is sewn so that it has a maximum opening of 75 inches at one end and flares to a maximum opening of 96 inches at the other. The material should be durable, weatherproof and not cling excessively to itself when wet. A material used for boat covers, called "pack cloth," is a good choice. Since the chute is difficult to make, I recommend that you buy it. A source is listed in Appendix B.

Barrels work well for the rigid opening of the tunnel. Plastic barrels are ideal since they are strong, resilient and can withstand the elements. You may obtain one from a company that manufactures barrels for chemical storage. The inner diameter of the barrel should be between 18 inches and 20 inches, and its standing height should be no more than 30 inches. Try to find one that has a removable lid. Cut off the bottom. (Because of the design of our barrel, cutting off the bottom was a tedious process involving a keyhole saw, but the result was well worth the effort.)

- First, mount the feet on the bottom of the plywood, and then mount the barrel. Since removing the bottom of the barrel reduces its rigidity, a 2" × 4" frame is required to keep it from deforming. The exact length of the 2" × 4"s will depend on the outer diameter of your barrel.
- To provide a nonslip walking surface for the dogs, attach an 8-inch-wide band of adhesive-backed, nonslip tape to the inside bottom of the barrel. You may need to use two strips of 4-inch-wide tape, which you can probably find at a local home-improvement store.
- How you attach the chute to the barrel will depend on the barrel you use. Most plastic barrels have a rim at the top. If this is true for your barrel, you can pass the front opening of the chute over the rim, secure it with a nylon strap and then fold the excess chute material over the strap. You could also sew a channel for the strap in the front of the

COLLAPSED TUNNEL

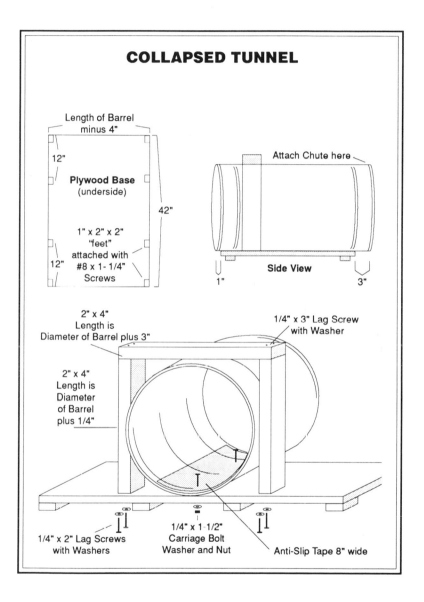

Length of Barrel minus 4"

12"

Plywood Base
(underside)

42"

1" x 2" x 2"
"feet"
attached with
#8 x 1- 1/4"
Screws

12"

Attach Chute here

Side View

1"

3"

2" x 4"
Length is
Diameter of Barrel plus 3"

1/4" x 3" Lag Screw
with Washer

2" x 4"
Length is
Diameter
of Barrel
plus 1/4"

1/4" x 2" Lag Screws
with Washers

1/4" x 1-1/2"
Carriage Bolt
Washer and Nut

Anti-Slip Tape 8" wide

207

chute. Nylon straps with buckles are readily available at hardware or variety stores.

Pipe Tunnel

Materials:

  6 ea.   4" × 4" × 16"
24 ea.   1" × 2" × 8"
48 ea.   #8 × 1-1½" wood screws

Tunnels are usually constructed of a flexible material attached to a spiraled wire frame. You can buy inexpensive play tunnels at some toy stores, although these usually have a not-so-durable plastic fabric decorated in a pattern appropriate for a child.

If you plan to use such tunnels for any length of time, you may want to remove the plastic and cover the wire frame with a more durable material. At this time you could attach two wire frames (by binding them together with wire or duct tape) to create a longer tunnel; this may be necessary to meet the USDAA length requirement for tunnels. Placing the new material over the frame is somewhat tricky, but it can be simplified if you use a Velcro seam. If you add up the cost of the play tunnels, a good weatherproof fabric and the Velcro, and then consider the effort involved in sewing, you may decide to buy the "Cadillac" of tunnels. This tunnel is not actually sold as a tunnel, but as a mineshaft ventilation duct. It is heavy-duty, long-lasting and very flexible.

Once you have a tunnel, you will need a means of holding it in place in the midst of wind and energized dogs. This is easily accomplished with stands constructed from 4" × 4"s and 1" × 2"s. Six stands per tunnel should be enough.

Number Markers

Materials:

5" vinyl numbers:
12 ea.   "1"
 3 ea.   "2"
 2 ea   "0", "3"–"9"
(Note: You may need to adjust the lengths of the 1" × 4"s and 1" × 6"s to accommodate the width of your numbers.)
 9 ea.   1" × 4" × 3-½" (small base)
10 ea.   1" × 4" × 6" (medium base)
 1 ea.   1" × 4" × 7" (large base)
 9 ea.   1" × 6" × 3-½" (small upright)
10 ea.   1" × 6" × 6" (medium upright)
 1 ea.   1" × 6" × 7" (large upright)
40 ea.   #8 × 1-½" wood screws

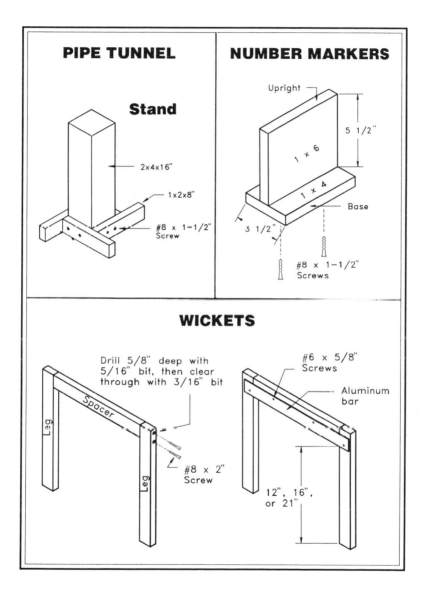

PIPE TUNNEL

Stand

2x4x16"

1x2x8"

#8 x 1-1/2"
Screw

NUMBER MARKERS

Upright

5 1/2"

1 x 6

1 x 4

Base

3 1/2"

#8 x 1-1/2"
Screws

WICKETS

Drill 5/8" deep with
5/16" bit, then clear
through with 3/16" bit

Spacer

Leg

Leg

#8 x 2"
Screw

#6 x 5/8"
Screws

Aluminum
bar

12", 16",
or 21"

Courses with obstacles that must be performed in order require number markers placed next to the obstacles. Since up to twenty obstacles may be used in a course, you must have numbers from 1 to 20. If you ever plan to have a Pairs Relay, you may want to have two sets of differently colored numbers so that both handlers can easily identify their individual portions of the course.

It is also necessary to delineate the start and finish lines. This can be done easily with orange traffic cones (two per line), which can be obtained from fire and safety supply stores. Of course, other markers are also possible; for example, you may prefer to use plywood cutouts of dogs.

The best way to put numbers on your markers is with adhesive-backed vinyl numbers, which are readily available. These are easy to apply and keep clean. Numbers 5 inches high work well. Only put numbers on one side of the marker so it will be clear in which direction the obstacle is to be performed.

The simplest markers are merely small orange traffic cones with vinyl numbers applied. However, the curved nature of the cones makes it difficult to read the numbers. Wooden markers are easy to make by screwing two pieces of wood together. Three different widths of markers are required, small ones for numbers 1 to 9, medium ones for numbers 10 to 19 and a large one for number 20.

Wickets

Materials:

2 ea.	$1'' \times 2'' \times 14\text{-}\frac{1}{4}''$ (small legs)
2 ea.	$1'' \times 2'' \times 18\text{-}\frac{1}{4}''$ (medium legs)
2 ea.	$1'' \times 2'' \times 23\text{-}\frac{1}{4}''$ (large legs)
1 ea.	$1'' \times 2'' \times 12''$ (small spacer)
1 ea.	$1'' \times 2'' \times 16''$ (medium spacer)
1 ea.	$1'' \times 2'' \times 20''$ (large spacer)
1 ea.	$\frac{1}{8}'' \times 1\text{-}\frac{1}{2}'' \times 15''$ aluminum bar
1 ea.	$\frac{1}{8}'' \times 1\text{-}\frac{1}{2}'' \times 19''$ aluminum bar
1 ea.	$\frac{1}{8}'' \times 1\text{-}\frac{1}{2}'' \times 23''$ aluminum bar
12 ea.	$\#8 \times 2''$ wood screws
12 ea.	$\#6 \times \frac{5}{8}''$ pan head sheet metal screws

Since the difference between the jump heights is so great (6 inches), it is crucial to measure the heights of dogs accurately. This is best done with wickets of fixed height. Wickets are U-shaped devices that are placed over the dog's withers (shoulders). If both legs of the wickets are able to touch the ground without your pushing down on the wicket, the dog is deemed to be shorter than the height of the wicket.

Screw the two legs to the spacer and drill the appropriate holes in the aluminum bar. Then mark the desired wicket height on each leg and screw the bar onto the wooden frame at the marked location. The aluminum bar provides

210

an accurate straightedge, is minimally affected by long hair and can be accurately positioned. Included here are details for three wickets designed for the four USDAA jump heights.

Hurdles

Hurdles can be divided into three types: long jumps, high jumps and spread jumps. Although several different types of long jumps are possible, including a water jump, the one detailed here is by far the most common in the United States. Obedience broad jumps can also be used if vertical poles are placed at each corner.

Unlike long jumps, high jumps are made in a large variety of styles, including bar jumps, solid (board) jumps, bone jumps and lattice jumps. Despite their differences, these hurdles have the same basic components: crosspieces that the dog jumps, supports on which the crosspieces rest, wings that hold the supports at the proper height and stands that keep the wings upright.

The solid Obedience high jump is not acceptable as an Agility high jump since there is no displaceable top piece. Besides making it difficult to penalize dogs that don't clear the jump cleanly, it is also a safety hazard to dogs that are running at full speed. Obedience bar jumps are acceptable, but the stands should be turned so that the bar can be displaced by a dog jumping in either direction.

The most common spread jumps are the double-bar jump and the triple-bar jump. The double-bar jump consists of two bars at the same jump height, about 12 inches apart, whereas the triple-bar jump consists of three bars placed at gradually increasing heights, with each bar spaced about 12 inches (horizontally) from the next. Although these jumps are sometimes constructed as one integral piece, it is recommended that you create them by placing several Standard single bar jumps together. This gives you more flexibility in designing the hurdle, and when you're not using a spread jump, you have several extra single-bar jumps you can use.

Here are designs for some of the most common hurdles that are now being used in the United States. Although there is a specific type of crosspiece to each hurdle (bar or board), there is no reason you can't use a different type of crosspiece; just make sure to use "bar supports" with bars and "board supports" with boards. You can create as many different types of hurdles as your imagination allows.

Long Jump

Materials:

4 ea.	1″ × 6″ × 6″, cut as shown (small side support)	1 ea.	1″ × 6″ × 60″	
		10 ea.	1″ × 2″ × 5-½″	
		2 ea.	¾″ × 48″ PVC pipe	

LONG JUMP

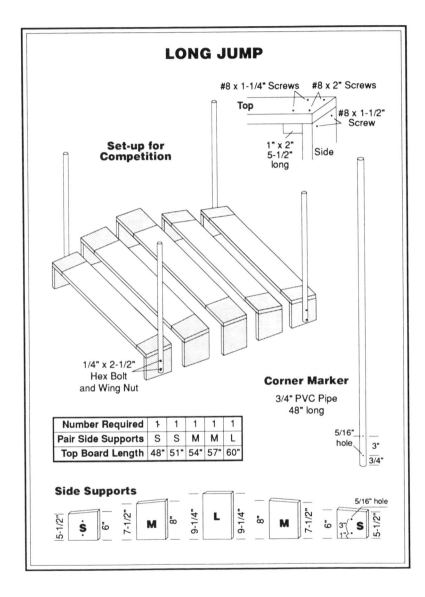

Set-up for Competition

#8 x 1-1/4" Screws   #8 x 2" Screws

Top

#8 x 1-1/2" Screw

1" x 2"
5-1/2"
long

Side

1/4" x 2-1/2"
Hex Bolt
and Wing Nut

Corner Marker

3/4" PVC Pipe
48" long

5/16"
hole

3"

3/4"

Number Required	1	1	1	1	1
Pair Side Supports	S	S	M	M	L
Top Board Length	48"	51"	54"	57"	60"

Side Supports

5-1/2" **S** 6"

7-1/2" **M** 8"

9-1/4" **L** 9-1/4"

8" **M** 7-1/2"

5/16" hole

6" 3" **S** 5-1/2" 1"

4 ea.	1″ × 6″ × 8″, cut as shown (medium side support)	20 ea.	#8 × 1-¼″ wood screws
2 ea.	1″ × 6″ × 9-¼″ (large side support)	20 ea.	#8 × 1-½″ wood screws
1 ea.	1″ × 6″ × 48″	20 ea.	#8 × 2″ wood screws
1 ea.	1″ × 6″ × 51″	8 ea.	¼″ × 2-½″ hex bolts
1 ea.	1″ × 6″ × 54″	8 ea.	¼″ wing nuts
1 ea.	1″ × 6″ × 57″		

The long jump consists of five jump boards, each of which consists of two side supports and one top board. This design differs from the Obedience broad jump in that for Agility the highest board is in the middle of the jump, so that the dog has the same sight picture regardless of the direction.

- Cut the side supports, which are three different sizes, and drill holes in the four smallest ones for the corner markers.
- Cut the top boards and use the table on page 212 to match them to the appropriate side supports.
- To assemble a jump board, screw one of the 1″ × 2″s on each end of a top board, and then screw the side supports to the 1″ × 2″s.
- Finally, flip the board over and screw the top board to the side supports.
- The jump boards are often painted two different colors; the side supports and ends of the top board are painted a dark color, while the centers of the top board are painted a light color.

Standard Single-Bar Jump

Materials:

2 ea.	Wings
4 ea.	Stands
4 ea.	Bars
10 ea.	Bar Supports

This is the "workhorse" hurdle. It's easy to make and is well suited for creating spread jumps. It consists of two wings, four stands, ten bar supports and four bars. Use an extra set of bar supports so that a bar can be positioned 6 inches off the ground, which is necessary when arranging spread jumps for the smaller jump heights. The 1″ × 2″ on the top of each wing, which prevents misguided dogs from skewering themselves on the upright 1″ × 4″s, also serves as a handle. The materials list and assembly directions are given separately for the wings, stands, bar supports and bars since many of these components can be used in other hurdles.

STANDARD SINGLE-BAR JUMP

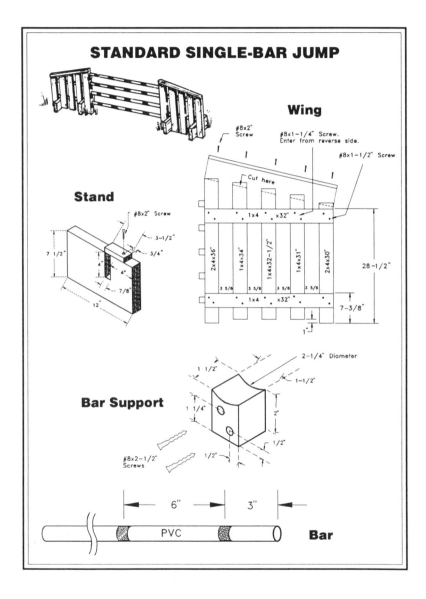

Wing

#8x2" Screw

#8x1-1/4" Screw.
Enter from reverse side.

#8x1-1/2" Screw

Cut here

1x4 x32"

2x4x36" 1x4x34" 1x4x32-1/2" 1x4x31" 2x4x30"

3 5/8   3 5/8   3 5/8   3 5/8

1x4 x32"

28-1/2"

7-3/8"

1"

Stand

#8x2" Screw

3-1/2"

3/4"

7 1/2"

4"

4"

7/8"

12"

Bar Support

2-1/4" Diameter

1 1/2"

1-1/2"

1 1/4"

2"

1/2"

#8x2-1/2"
Screws

1/2"

Bar

6"   3"

PVC

Materials for two wings:

2 ea.   2″ × 4″ × 36″
2 ea.   2″ × 4″ × 30″
2 ea.   1″ × 4″ × 34″
2 ea.   1″ × 4″ × 32-½″
4 ea.   1″ × 4″ × 32″
2 ea.   1″ × 4″ × 31″
2 ea.   1″ × 2″ × 32 ⅝″
24 ea. #8 × 1-¼″ wood screws
16 ea. #8 × 1-½″ wood screws
10 ea. #8 × 2″ wood screws
20 ea. #8 × 2-½″ wood screws

- Lay out the two 2″ × 4″s and the two 1″ × 4″ × 32″s as they will be assembled.
- With a straightedge, mark a line from the the outer top corner of the 2″ × 4″ × 36″ to the same corner of the 2″ × 4″ × 30″.
- Trim the 2″ × 4″s along this line and screw the four boards together.
- Flip the assembly and lay the other 1″ × 4″s in position.
- Use the straightedge to mark the same line as before, cut the 1″ × 4″s and screw them in position.
- Then screw the 1″ × 2″ onto the top.
- Finally, attach the bar supports. When making the second wing, be sure it is the mirror image of the first.

STAND

Materials for four stands:

4 ea.   2″ × 8″ × 12″
4 ea.   1″ × 2″ × 3-½″
4 ea.   #8 × 2″ wood screws

The stands keep the wings from falling over. Two are required for each wing —four for a complete jump. The stands are designed to attach to and detach from the wings in seconds. When attached, the wings and stand can be conveniently moved as one unit. Detaching the stands allows the wings and stands to be packed efficiently for storage or transportation.

- Cut the slot with a band saw or saber saw. Cutting the slot is simplified if you first drill a hole at each corner of the slot so that the direction of the saw blade can be changed at the corner.
- Then place the 1″ × 2″ in position, drill a hole through the 1″ × 2″ and into the 2″ × 8″ with a pilot bit and screw down the 1″ × 2″. Don't screw down too tightly since the 1″ × 2″ must be able to pivot.

The bar supports are made from 2″ × 2″s. They are designed so that bars can be easily placed at all of the jump heights, even when the wings are sitting on uneven terrain.

- Cut an arc in the support so that the bar will not be displaced by a breeze. It should not be too deep, however, since the bar needs to be easily displaceable if a dog hits it. The simplest way to cut the arc is with a band saw, but you will have to use a ¼-inch or thinner blade. If the cut is rough, you will need to smooth the arc with a rasp. You can make better cuts with a hole saw and a drill press, but this is much more difficult and tedious.
- Attach the bar supports with two #8 × 2-½″ wood screws so that the tops of the bars are at the proper heights: 6 inches, 12 inches, 18 inches, 24 inches and 30 inches. (The 6-inch positions are used when the jump is part of a spread-bar hurdle.)

BARS

Bars are the most common crosspieces, probably because they are inexpensive and easy to make. Simply cut a 10-foot length of PVC pipe into two 5-foot bars. I recommend using 1-inch PVC rated to 160 or 200 psi, which is light and inexpensive. To improve appearance, you can remove the ink on the PVC with acetone.

Wrap colored plastic tape around the bars to form stripes. The tape is important to help the dog see the bar, and its color should be chosen to provide a high contrast with the bar. Alternatively, you can wrap the entire length of PVC with strips of tape in alternating colors. Keep in mind that dogs are more or less color-blind and have trouble distinguishing between some colors, such as green and yellow.

Fan Jump

Materials:

2 ea.	Wings
4 ea.	Stands
4 ea.	Boards
8 ea.	Board Supports

The fan jump derives its name from the orientation of the uprights in the wing, which fan out from one area. It can be a very beautiful and stylish jump, particularly when the uprights are painted different colors, and it is not much harder to make than the standard jump. It uses the same wing stands described for the standard bar jump. However, it uses boards and "board supports," rather

216

FAN JUMP and BARREL JUMP

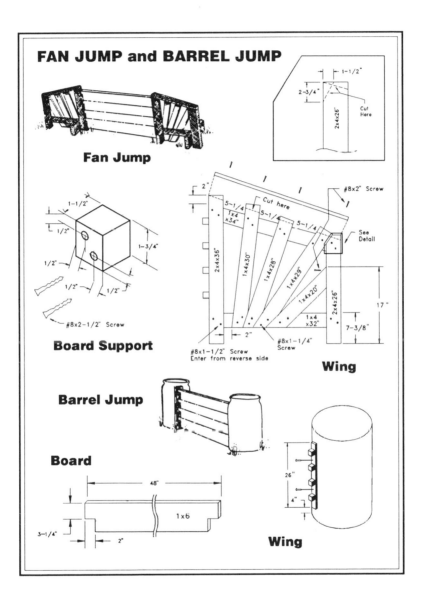

Fan Jump

2-3/4"   1-1/2"

2x4x26"   Cut Here

Board Support

1-1/2"
1/2"
1-3/4"
1/2"
1/2"   1/2"

#8x2-1/2" Screw

#8x2" Screw

2"   Cut here
5-1/4"   1x4 x34"   5-1/4"   5-1/4"

2x4x35"   1x4x30"   1x4x28"   1x4x29"   1x4x20"   2x4x26"   See Detail

1x4 x32"   17"
7-3/8"

2"   #8x1-1/4" Screw

#8x1-1/2" Screw
Enter from reverse side

Wing

Barrel Jump

Board

48"
1x6
3-1/4"   2"

26"
4"

Wing

than bars and "bar supports." The materials and assembly instructions for the boards and board supports are listed separately.

WING

Materials for two wings:

2 ea.   2″ × 4″ × 36″
2 ea.   2″ × 4″ × 26″
2 ea.   1″ × 4″ × 34″
2 ea.   1″ × 4″ × 32″
2 ea.   1″ × 4″ × 30″
2 ea.   1″ × 4″ × 29″
2 ea.   1″ × 4″ × 28″
2 ea.   1″ × 4″ × 20″
2 ea.   1″ × 2″ × 33¾″
28 ea. #8 × 1-¼″ wood screws
16 ea. #8 × 1-½″ wood screws
10 ea. #8 × 2″ wood screws
16 ea. #8 × 2-½″ wood screws

The wings are constructed in a fashion very similar to those of the standard bar jump.

- Mark the required cuts to the top of the 2″ × 4″ × 26″ and make the cuts.
- Then lay out the two 2″ × 4″s, the 1″ × 4″ × 32″, and the 1″ × 4″ × 34″.
- Using a straightedge, mark a line from the outer top corner of the 2″ × 4″ × 36″ to the top of the 2″ × 4″ × 26″. Also mark the 1″ × 4″ × 34″ along the edges of the 2″ × 4″s. Then cut along these lines.
- Screw these four pieces together and flip the assembly.
- Lay the 1″ × 4″ × 30″ in the indicated position. The 2-inch space between the 2″ × 4″ × 36″ and the 1″ × 4″ × 30″ is required for the stand.
- Lay a straightedge along the tops of the 2″ × 4″s and draw a line on the 1″ × 4″ × 30″. Draw another line marking the bottom of the 1″ × 4″ × 32″.
- Then lay the 1″ × 4″ × 28″ in place, overlaying the 1″ × 4″ × 30″, and use it to draw a line on the 1″ × 4″ × 30″.
- Make the three cuts in the 1″ × 4″ × 30″ and screw it in place.
- Follow the same procedure with the 1″ × 4″ × 28″ and 1″ × 4″ × 29″.
- Then mark the 1″ × 4″ × 20″ with this procedure, drill the hole for the #8 screw on its edge and screw the bottom in place.

- To insert the top screw, you will have to temporarily remove the 1″ × 4″ × 29″.
- Finally, attach the top piece and add the bar supports. When making the second wing, be sure it is the mirror image of the first.

BOARDS

Boards are used to give the impression of a solid wall. They must be shorter than the jump-height increment and balanced so they can be easily displaced if a dog bumps them. Because of their mass, they are usually harder to displace than PVC bars, so it is best to use the minimum length (and hence the minimum weight) allowed. The best appearance is obtained when there is a minimum amount of gap between the boards, so try 1″ × 6″ boards. Four boards are required for each hurdle.

Since boards have a large surface area, they can be blown off hurdles by high winds. Thus, you should have enough bar jumps to be able to substitute them for board jumps at outdoor competitions.

BOARD SUPPORTS

These are similar to the bar supports described for the standard single-bar jump, except that they are slightly shorter and don't have an arc.

Barrel Jump

Materials:

2 ea. barrels
2 ea. 1″ × 2″ × 26″
4 ea. Boards
8 ea. Board Supports

The barrel jump is easy to make and adds variety to your hurdles. Buy two barrels that are at least 36 inches tall. Plastic barrels are best since they are lightweight and weatherproof. Mount a 1″ × 2″ to each barrel to hold the board supports. The boards and board supports are identical to those described for the fan jump.

Bone Jump

Bone jumps are very appealing to the audience. The jump consists of a crossbar shaped like a bone, and it is supported by wings shaped like dogs. Of course, everyone wants the wings to resemble their favorite breed, so there is a wide variety of bone jumps around the country.

Because these hurdles have to accommodate several jump heights and the wings generally have curved shapes, it is usually necessary to attach the board supports to one of the wing faces instead of to the edge. Consequently, the bone jump should only be jumped in one direction.

- Cut the dogs from ¾-inch plywood.
- Make the straight portion of the bone at least four feet long.
- The bone should also have 2-inch-wide "handles" sticking out from each end to support the bone.
- The handles should be about 14 inches long, depending on your wing design.
- Cut the bone and handles from one piece of ¾-inch plywood or a 1″ × 10″.
- Paint the handles a different color than the rest of the board to make the bone look like a "bone."
- Bolt the dogs to 2″ × 4″ stands in such a way that the wings do not contact the ground.

Lattice Jump

Building the lattice jump is very time-consuming and trickier than you might think, although it is impressive when you are finished.

Since the lattice is usually painted a different color than the frame, and since it is susceptible to breaking, the lattice needs to be easy to remove from the frame. If the crosspiece is to be knocked over easily, it must be supported at the bottom rather than the top. However, it should not be so unstable that it falls off on its own, so center the lattice inside the frame. Since painting the jump is also involved, it is recommended that you don't build this jump until you have finished all of your other equipment.

An outline of the procedure is as follows:

- Use 1″ × 2″s to build frames for the lattice, with the edges of the 1″ × 2″s facing the approaching dog.
- Screw ½″ × ¾″ rectangular molding along the edge of the inside of the frame to form a lip.
- Place the lattice inside the frame against the lip.
- Secure it in place by screwing more of the same molding to the lip so that the lattice is sandwiched between the molding.
- Screw a 1″ × 4″ across the bottom instead of extending the lattice of the wings all the way to the ground. This way, the same stands described for the standard single-bar jump and fan jump can be used. The bottom of the crosspiece frame should extend 2 inches past the sides so that it can be supported by the board supports.
- Make two crosspieces that are 10 inches high; only one will be used for 12-inch and 18-inch jump heights, and two will be used for 24-inch and 30-inch jump heights.

A-FRAME

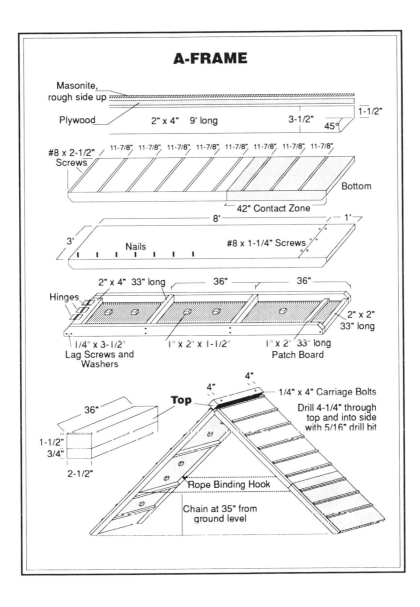

Masonite, rough side up

Plywood

2" x 4" 9' long 3-1/2"

1-1/2"

45°

#8 x 2-1/2" Screws

11-7/8" 11-7/8" 11-7/8" 11-7/8" 11-7/8" 11-7/8" 11-7/8" 11-7/8"

Bottom

42" Contact Zone

8' 1'

3'

Nails

#8 x 1-1/4" Screws

2" x 4" 33" long 36" 36"

Hinges

2" x 2" 33" long

1/4" x 3-1/2" Lag Screws and Washers

1" x 2" x 1-1/2"

1" x 2" 33" long Patch Board

4"

36"

Top

4"

4"

1/4" x 4" Carriage Bolts

Drill 4-1/4" through top and into side with 5/16" drill bit

1-1/2"
3/4"

2-1/2"

Rope Binding Hook

Chain at 35" from ground level

221

Contact Obstacles

A-Frame

Materials:

4 ea.	2″ × 4″ × 9′, cut as shown (rails of wall)
6 ea.	2″ × 4″ × 33″ (rail dividers)
2 ea.	2″ × 2″ × 33″
1 ea.	2″ × 4″ × 36″, cut as shown (top)
1 ea.	1″ × 4″ × 36″, cut as shown (top)
2 ea.	1″ × 2″ × 33″ (patch board)
18 ea.	1″ × 2″ × 36″ (antislip slats)
10 ea.	1″ × 2″ × 1-½″
2 ea.	3′ × 8′ of ½″ plywood
2 ea.	3′ × 1′ of ½″ plywood
2 ea.	3′ × 8′ of ¼″ Masonite
2 ea.	3′ × 1′ of ¼″ Masonite
28 ea.	¼″ × 3-½″ lag screws
28 ea.	¼″ washers
2 ea.	¼″ × 4″ carriage bolts
12 ea.	#8 × 1¼″ screws
60 ea.	#8 × 2-½″ wood screws
1 box	8D ringed nails
4 ea.	rope binding hooks
8 ea.	#12 × 1″ machine screws (for rope binding hooks)
3 ea.	3-½″ door hinges with removable pins
14 ft.	2/0 tenso chain
4 ft.	2/0 tenso chain (optional)
2 ea.	removable chain repair links
	wood glue

This design makes a very strong A-frame that can withstand use at the low heights required for introductory training. It consists of two walls and a top. To build an A-frame:

- Assemble the frame.
- Then position the plywood over the frame and the Masonite on top of the plywood (rough side up), and nail them both to the frame using ringed nails.
- Since the frame is 9 feet long and plywood and Masonite come in 8-foot lengths, you will have a seam; put the seams from both the plywood and Masonite 1 foot from the bottom of the wall.
- After nailing, place a 1″ × 2″ patch board under the seam and screw through the Masonite and plywood into the 1″ × 2″ to strengthen the seam.

- Glue 1" × 2" × 1-½" squares on the bottom of the walls so that screws passing through the centers of the antislip slats will pass through the squares.
- Screw on the antislip slats.
- After both walls are made, lay them on the ground with the underside facing up and the two tops touching, and attach the hinges.
- Raise the A-frame up until it is 6 feet 3 inches high, and attach the rope binding hooks 35 inches off the ground.
- Next, cut the chain into two lengths to keep the A-frame at this height.
- The top is made by ripping a 1" × 4" and a 2" × 4" to the proper widths and gluing them together. It is pinned to the top of the A-frame with carriage bolts.
- Paint a yellow 42-inch-long contact zone on the lower end of each wall.

When training beginning dogs, you will probably find it useful to lower the height of the A-frame. To do this, remove the top and add extra lengths of chain to the main chains, using removable repair links. Be sure to put another board on the top so that dogs' paws don't get caught.

Dog Walk

Materials:

8 ea.	2" × 4" × 43" (stand legs)
4 ea.	1" × 4" × 21" (stand)
4 ea.	1" × 4" × 13", cut as shown (stand)
2 ea.	2" × 4" × 23" (top-plank support)
2 ea.	2" × 2" × 23" (top-plank support)
2 ea.	2" × 2" × 6", cut to 1" × 1" × 6" (side-plank support)
2 ea.	2" × 4" × 11' 11-¼" (top plank rail)
4 ea.	2" × 4" × 11' 11-¼", cut as shown (side plank rail)
10 ea.	2" × 4" × 6-⅜"
2 ea.	2" × 4" × 6-⅜", cut as shown (top end piece of side plank)
2 ea.	⅜" plywood, 9-⅜" × 41-¾" (side plank)
2 ea.	⅜" plywood, 9-⅜" × 53-¾" (side plank)
5 ea.	⅜" plywood, 9-⅜" × 47-¾" (side plank and top plank)
24 ea.	1" × 2" × 9-¼" (antislip slats)
32 ea.	#6 × ⅝" pan head sheet metal screws
16 ea.	#8 × 1-½" wood screws
52 ea.	#8 × 2-½" wood screws
4 ea.	#8 × 2-½" wood screws
32 ea.	¼" × 3-½" lag screws
6 ea.	¼" × 3" lag screws
38 ea.	¼" washers
4 ea.	¼" × 3-½" carriage bolts

DOG WALK

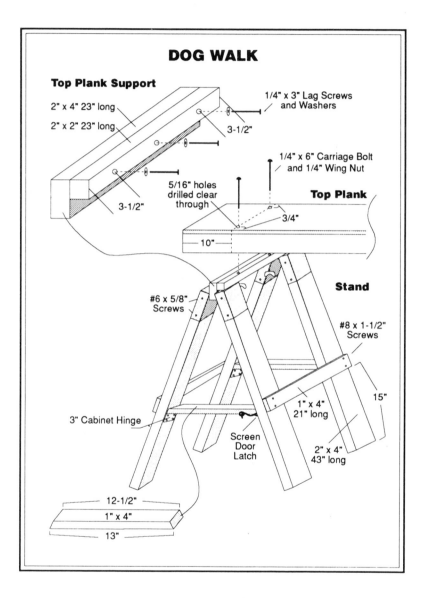

Top Plank Support

2" x 4" 23" long

2" x 2" 23" long

1/4" x 3" Lag Screws and Washers

3-1/2"

1/4" x 6" Carriage Bolt and 1/4" Wing Nut

5/16" holes drilled clear through

3-1/2"

Top Plank

3/4"

10"

Stand

#6 x 5/8" Screws

#8 x 1-1/2" Screws

15"

1" x 4" 21" long

3" Cabinet Hinge

Screen Door Latch

2" x 4" 43" long

12-1/2"

1" x 4"

13"

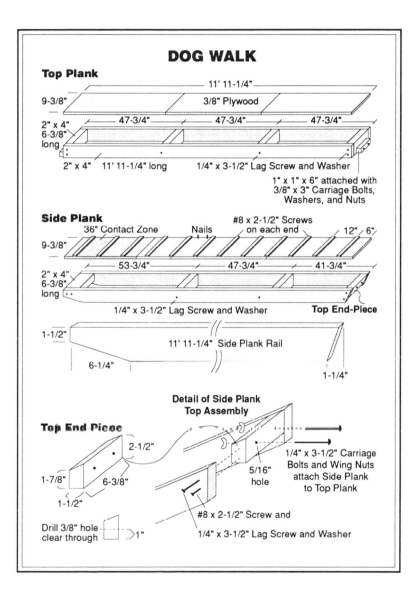

DOG WALK

Top Plank

11' 11-1/4"

9-3/8"

3/8" Plywood

2" x 4"
6-3/8"
long

47-3/4"   47-3/4"   47-3/4"

2" x 4"   11' 11-1/4" long   1/4" x 3-1/2" Lag Screw and Washer

1" x 1" x 6" attached with
3/8" x 3" Carriage Bolts,
Washers, and Nuts

Side Plank

36" Contact Zone   Nails   #8 x 2-1/2" Screws
on each end   12" 6"

9-3/8"

2" x 4"
6-3/8"
long

53-3/4"   47-3/4"   41-3/4"

1/4" x 3-1/2" Lag Screw and Washer   **Top End-Piece**

1-1/2"

11' 11-1/4" Side Plank Rail

6-1/4"

1-1/4"

**Detail of Side Plank
Top Assembly**

Top End Piece

2-1/2"

1-7/8"   6-3/8"

1-1/2"

5/16"
hole

1/4" x 3-1/2" Carriage
Bolts and Wing Nuts
attach Side Plank
to Top Plank

Drill 3/8" hole
clear through   1"

#8 x 2-1/2" Screw and

1/4" x 3-1/2" Lag Screw and Washer

4 ea.	¼" × 6" carriage bolts
8 ea.	¼" wing nuts
1 box	1-¼" ringed nails
4 ea.	⅜" × 3" carriage bolts
4 ea.	⅜" washers
4 ea.	⅜" nuts
4 ea.	screen door latches
4 ea.	3" cabinet hinges
4 ea.	heavy-duty sawhorse brackets

The dog walk consists of two stands, two side planks and a top plank. The top plank is bolted to the stands, while the side planks are bolted to the top plank. The top end piece of the side planks rest on a 1" × 1" × 6" piece of wood that is bolted to the top plank, and each is held in place by two bolts.

- Assemble the stands. You will probably have to drill bigger holes in the sawhorse brackets to accept the #6 screws.
- Assemble the top plank and bolt it to the stands.
- Drill the holes in a top end piece of one of the side planks, and use it as a template to drill the corresponding holes in both ends of the top plank.
- Use the holes in one end of the top plank as a template to drill the holes in the second end piece. The two side planks will now be interchangeable.
- Finally, bolt both end pieces to the top plank and construct the side planks about the end pieces.
- Paint the obstacle, using sand paint on the walking surfaces, as described in the next section. Paint the bottom 36 inches of each plank yellow to signify the contact zones.

Cross-Over

Materials:

4 ea.	2" × 4" × 30-½" (tabletop)
1 ea.	½" plywood, 32" × 32" (tabletop)
4 ea.	2" × 8" × 51" (table legs)
4 ea.	2" × 2" × 3", cut 2 triangles from each, as shown
4 ea.	2" × 2" × 6", cut to 1-⅛" × 1-⅛" × 6" (plank supports)
1 pc.	46" × 46" outdoor carpeting
1 box	9⁄16" staples
8 ea.	¼" × 3-½" lag screws
8 ea.	¼" flat washers
8 ea.	⅜" × 3" carriage bolts
8 ea.	⅜" washers
8 ea.	⅜" nuts
8 ea.	½" × 10" carriage bolts

CROSS-OVER

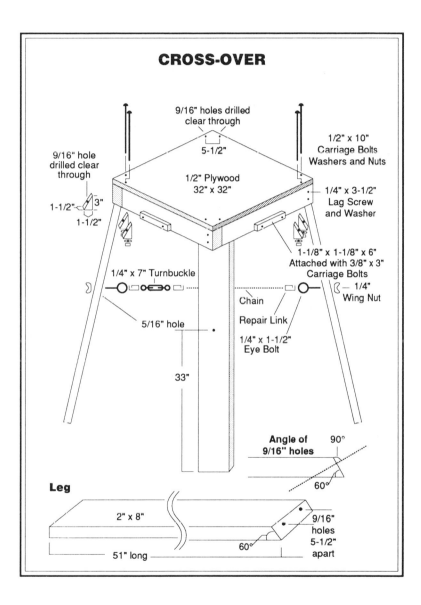

9/16" holes drilled clear through

5-1/2"

1/2" x 10" Carriage Bolts Washers and Nuts

9/16" hole drilled clear through

1-1/2" — 3"

1-1/2"

1/2" Plywood 32" x 32"

1/4" x 3-1/2" Lag Screw and Washer

1-1/8" x 1-1/8" x 6" Attached with 3/8" x 3" Carriage Bolts

1/4" x 7" Turnbuckle

1/4" Wing Nut

Chain

Repair Link

5/16" hole

1/4" x 1-1/2" Eye Bolt

33"

Angle of 9/16" holes   90°

60°

Leg

2" x 8"

9/16" holes 5-1/2" apart

60°

51" long

227

8 ea.	½″ flat washers
8 ea.	½″ nuts
4 ea.	¼″ × 1-½″ eye bolts
4 ea.	¼″ wing nuts
8 ft.	⅖ tenso chain
6 ea.	chain repair links
2 ea.	¼″ × 7″ eye-to-eye turnbuckles
4 ea.	side planks as in dog walk (materials listed below):
8 ea.	2″ × 4″ × 11′ 11-¼″ (plank rail, cut as shown)
12 ea.	2″ × 4″ × 6-⅜″
4 ea.	2″ × 4″ × 6-⅜″ (top end piece of side plank, cut as shown)
4 ea.	⅜″ plywood, 9-⅜″ × 41-¾″ (side plank)
4 ea.	⅜″ plywood, 9-⅜″ × 53-¾″ (side plank)
4 ea.	⅜″ plywood, 9-⅜″ × 47-¾″ (side plank and top plank)
48 ea.	1″ × 2″ × 9-¼″ (antislip slats)
104 ea.	#8 × 2-½″ wood screws
40 ea.	¼″ × 3-½″ lag screws
40 ea.	¼″ flat washers
8 ea.	¼″ × 3-½″ carriage bolts
8 ea.	¼″ wing nuts
1 box	1-¼″ ringed nails

The crossover consists of a table and four planks. One of the best features of this design is that the resultant crossover is easy to use. It can be assembled and disassembled by one person. The legs remain in a fixed position, so the table is easier to move and level than those with legs that can swing freely. Furthermore, the planks are identical to those used with the dog walk, and are easy to attach and remove since they rest on ledges while wing nuts are screwed to two bolts.

Construct the table top in the same manner as the 24-inch tabletop is constructed.

- Flip the tabletop and drill the holes for the legs through the 2″ × 4″ table frame, drilling as straight as possible.
- Cut the legs and drill the two holes in the top edge of each leg.
- Now make the triangular blocks by cutting four 3-inch lengths of 2″ × 2″ and drilling a 9/16″ hole down the center, lengthwise.
- Cut each piece into two triangles.
- Starting with the table top upside down, bolt the legs onto the table top.
- Flip the table over and attach the chains.
- Bolt on the four 1-⅛″ × 1-⅛″ × 6″ pieces.

Construct the planks using the design for the dog walk planks.

- So that planks will all be interchangeable, remove one of the planks from the dog walk, take the top end piece from one of the crossover

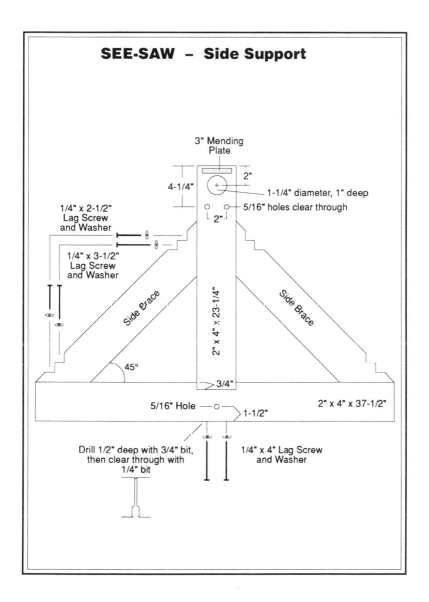

SEE-SAW – Side Support

3" Mending Plate

4-1/4"

2"

1-1/4" diameter, 1" deep

5/16" holes clear through

2"

1/4" x 2-1/2" Lag Screw and Washer

1/4" x 3-1/2" Lag Screw and Washer

Side Brace

Side Brace

2" x 4" x 23-1/4"

45°

3/4"

5/16" Hole

1-1/2"

2" x 4" x 37-1/2"

Drill 1/2" deep with 3/4" bit, then clear through with 1/4" bit

1/4" x 4" Lag Screw and Washer

SEE-SAW

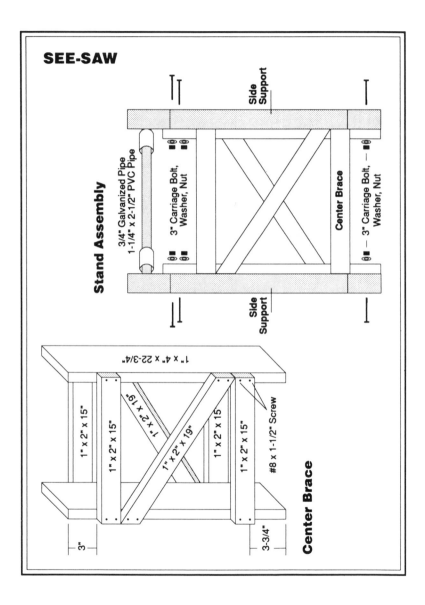

Stand Assembly

Side Support

3/4" Galvanized Pipe
1-1/4" x 2-1/2" PVC Pipe

3" Carriage Bolt, Washer, Nut

Center Brace

— 3" Carriage Bolt, Washer, Nut

Side Support

Center Brace

1" x 4" x 22-3/4"

1" x 2" x 15"

1" x 2" x 15"

1" x 2" x 19"

1" x 2" x 19"

1" x 2" x 15"

1" x 2" x 15"

#8 x 1-1/2" Screw

3"

3-3/4"

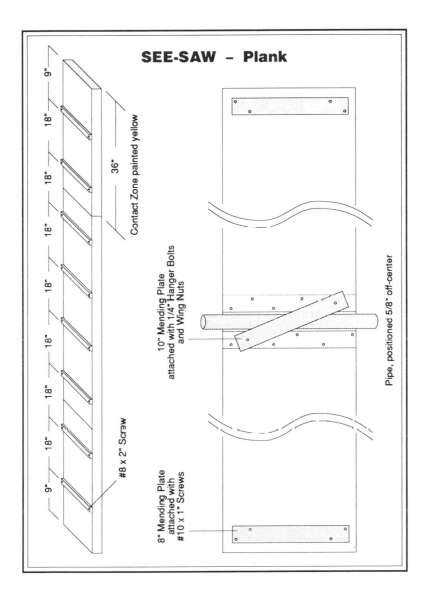

SEE-SAW – Plank

9" 18" 18" 18" 18" 18" 18" 18" 9"

36"

Contact Zone painted yellow

#8 x 2" Screw

8" Mending Plate
attached with
#10 x 1" Screws

10" Mending Plate
attached with 1/4" Hanger Bolts
and Wing Nuts

Pipe, positioned 5/8" off-center

planks and position it in the proper place on the dog walk, and use the holes in the end of the top plank as a template to drill the holes in the end piece.

- You can then use this end piece as a template for drilling the corresponding holes on the crossover. Holes for the other three top end pieces can be made using the holes drilled in the crossover.
- Bolt all four end pieces to the sides of the table and construct the planks about them.

Finally, remove the planks and legs from the crossover and cover the table top with outdoor carpeting. Staple the carpeting to the bottom of the frame. (The 1-⅛″ × 1-⅛″ × 6″ pieces should not be covered.) Cut holes in the carpet around the holes in the tabletop, and staple the carpet around all the holes.

Paint the obstacle, using sand paint on the walking surfaces, as described in the next section. Paint the bottom 36 inches of each plank yellow to signify the contact zones.

See-Saw

Materials:

2 ea.	2″ × 4″ × 37-½″ (side support)
2 ea.	2″ × 4″ × 23-¼″ (side support)
4 ea.	2″ × 4″ × 24″ cut as in diagram on page 229 (side braces)
2 ea.	1″ × 4″ × 22-¾″ (center brace)
4 ea.	1″ × 2″ × 15″ (center brace)
2 ea.	1″ × 2″ × 19″ (center brace)
8 ea.	1″ × 2″ × 9-¼″ (antislip slats)
2 ea.	2″ × 2″ × 9-¼″, cut to 1-½″ × ⅛″ more than pipe diameter (pipe positioner)
1 ea.	2″ × 10″ × 12′ (top plank)
1 ea.	¾″ galvanized steel pipe (1-⅛″ OD), 16-¾″ long
2 ea.	1-¼″ PVC pipe, 2-½″ long (optional)
1 ea.	10″ mending plate
2 ea.	8″ mending plates
2 ea.	3″ mending plates and screws
24 ea.	#8 × 1-½″ wood screws
18 ea.	#8 × 2″ wood screws
10 ea.	#10 × 2-½″ wood screws
8 ea.	#10 × 1″ flat head sheet metal screws (for 8″ mending plate)
2 ea.	¼″ hanger bolts
8 ea.	¼″ × 2-½″ lag screws
8 ea.	¼″ × 3-½″ lag screws
4 ea.	¼″ × 4″ lag screws
6 ea.	¼″ × 2-½″ carriage bolts

26 ea.   ¼″ washers
 6 ea.   ¼″ nuts
 2 ea.   ¼″ wing nuts

- Cut the pieces for the two side supports and drill the holes. The side brace of the support is detailed in the diagram on page 229, and the hole for the pipe should be drilled only 1 inch deep.
- Mount 3-inch mending plates above the hole for the pipe to prevent the wood from splitting.
- Assemble the side support, and then construct the center brace.
- Place the center brace against the side supports in the proper position for assembly, and drill 5⁄16-inch holes in the center brace using the holes in the side supports as guides.
- Bolt the side supports to the center brace, making sure to include the pipe.
- If you wish, you can place two 2-½-inch lengths of 1-¼-inch PVC pipe over the bar to help center the plank. Normally, you should not have to disassemble the stand.
- Screw the antislip slats on the top of the plank.
- Then flip it over and screw the 8-inch mending plates to the bottom ends of the plank. These help prevent the wood from splitting.
- Attach the 2″ × 2″s (cut as indicated in the materials list) that hold the plank in position about 5⁄8-inch off-center, so that the see-saw will have a "down" side. Space them slightly farther apart than the diameter of the pipe.
- Screw two hanger bolts into the 2″ × 2″s so as to line up with holes in the mending plate. To attach the hanger bolts, screw two nuts onto the bolt side and use a wrench to screw in the other side. Then remove the two nuts. The see-saw can now be placed over the pipe in the stand.
- Secure it to the pipe by screwing the mending plate over the pipe with wing nuts. You may have to trim the mending plate so it doesn't extend beyond the edges of the plank.
- Paint the obstacle, using sand paint on the walking surfaces, as described in the next section. Paint the bottom 36 inches of the plank ends yellow to signify the contact zones.

Painting

Painting can be very tedious and time-consuming, but it is necessary to protect your investment and provide an attractive appearance. Be sure to use a quality exterior paint. We prefer latex to oil paints since they can be cleaned up with water. We also prefer gloss to flat finishes, since they are easier to keep clean and look brighter. However, *do not use gloss on the walking surfaces of the contact obstacles* since it dries to a smooth, slippery surface.

Contact zones must be painted yellow, and the rest of the walking surface of the contact must be painted a contrasting color. Other than the yellow contact zones, you are free to choose your own colors. We have chosen two colors of a brand-name paint for our color scheme, so we can always buy more of the exact shades to touch up our old paint jobs. When choosing colors, remember that dogs have trouble distinguishing between green and yellow.

Your first coat of paint should be a primer, which helps the following coats adhere to the wood and helps hide the grain of the wood. Then follow with two coats of paint.

The walking surfaces of the dog walk, cross-over, and see-saw require special attention to provide proper traction for the dogs. We use "play" sand, which is used in children's sandboxes. First apply the primer and let it dry. Then apply your first coat of regular paint, and pour sand over the entire surface. After the paint has dried, remove the loose sand, either by turning the board upside down and tapping it, or by using a soft brush. Repeat this process two more times, and then put a final coat of paint over the sand.

APPENDIX B

Agility Resources

National Agility Organizations

United States Dog Agility Association (USDAA)
P.O. Box 850955
Richardson, TX 75085-0955
(214) 231-9700

National Club for Dog Agility (NCDA)
401 Bluemont Circle
Manhattan, KS 66502
(913) 537-7022

Collapsed Tunnel Chutes

Texas Canvas Products
728 S. Beltline Rd.
Irving, TX 75060
(214) 790-1501

Sturdy chute of nylon pack cloth, approximately 12 feet long with one end approximately 95 inches in circumference. Specify circumference of the other end to fit your rigid opening—allow several extra inches for flexibility.

Pipe Tunnels

ABC Peabody
P.O. Box 2928
Grand Junction, CO 81502
(303) 242-3664 west of Rockies
(219) 267-5166 east of Rockies

Industrial-strength pipe tunnels made of mine-shaft duct material. Specify that you would like a section of 24-inch diameter Mineduct in a 12-foot length.

Armbands, Dog Show Signs, Etc.

Kal Kan Foods
3250 E. 44th St.
Vernon, CA 90058
1-(800) 669-6393, ext. 4981

Cheap Sheets
5331 W. 53rd Pl.
Chicago, IL 60638
(312) 581-3490

Purina Show and Field Materials
P.O. Box 21982
Greensboro, NC 27420
1-(800) 648-3022

Lightweight Obedience Training Jumps

Lite-N-Qwik Fold Training Jumps
(Dog Owner's Guide)
P.O. Box 276
Harper, TX 78631
1-(800) 468-5867

J & J Dog Supplies
P.O. Box 1517
Galesburg, IL 61402
1-(800) 642-2050

Acme Jumps (Acme Machine Co.)
2901 Fremont Ave. South
Minneapolis, MN 55408
1-(800) 332-2472

Low-Cost Insurance For Nonprofit Dog Clubs

Sportsman's Insurance Plan for Dog Clubs
P.O. Box 43
Clayton, NY 13624
(315) 654-2068

Suggested Reading

The Agility Dog International. By Peter Lewis. Southampton, England: Canine Publications, 1988.
Agility Is Fun! By Ruth Hobday. Manchester, England: 'Our Dogs' Publishing Co., Ltd., 1989.

Beyond Basic Dog Training. By Diane L. Bauman. New York: Howell Book House, 1991.

Don't Shoot the Dog. By Karen Pryor. New York: Simon & Schuster, 1984.

Mother Knows Best—The Natural Way to Train Your Dog. By Carol Lea Benjamin. New York: Howell Book House, 1985.